INFLUENCE:
THE SECRET OF SELLING

Influence:

The Secret of Selling

Laban T. M'mbololo, Esq.

Copyright © 2019 by Laban T. M'mbololo, Esq.

ISBN: Softcover   978-1-9845-6252-4
           eBook   978-1-9845-6251-7

All rights reserved. No part of this book may be reproduced or transmitted in any form or by any means, electronic or mechanical, including photocopying, recording, or by any information storage and retrieval system, without permission in writing from the copyright owner.

The views expressed in this work are solely those of the author and do not necessarily reflect the views of the publisher, and the publisher hereby disclaims any responsibility for them.

Any people depicted in stock imagery provided by Getty Images are models, and such images are being used for illustrative purposes only.
Certain stock imagery © Getty Images.

Print information available on the last page.

Rev. date: 12/26/2018

To order additional copies of this book, contact:
Xlibris
1-888-795-4274
www.Xlibris.com
Orders@Xlibris.com
785935

Contents

About the Author vii
Acknowledgements xi
Dedication xiii
Foreword xv
Introduction xvii

Chapter 1: The Power of Attraction; Making The Prospects Come to You 1

Chapter 2: The Power of Differentiation; Setting You Apart From other Sales People 19

Chapter 3: The Power of Visibilty; Having More of the Right People in Front of You 25

Chapter 4: The Power of Credibility; Getting People to Trust You ... 38

Chapter 5: The Power of Authority; Getting Your Proposal Accepted and Being a Power Seller 46

Chapter 6: You Know You are at the Top When….. 71

Amplify Your Business 81
Epilogue: You are Now a Power Seller! 87

About the Author

Laban T. M'mbololo Esq. comes with a strong academic background with accreditations from the London Chamber of Commerce and Industry (LCCI), ASET, Oxford Cambridge and RSA (OCR) – London, U.K. and over 20 years stint in diverse business management, corporate sales, relationship management & sales leadership in banking, cross-border sourcing, offshore real estate & financing. Desire to explore new frontiers, travel, and learn international best practices replanted him in Dubai, a rapidly growing modern state and a force to reckon with as the dominant economic powerhouse within the Middle East region. He has also participated in *"Unleash the Power Within"* a very powerful and life changing seminar by Tony Robbins and attended peak performance coaching by Jean-Pierre De Villiers a London based international speaker and best-selling author.

Laban has over 10 years' International project experience gained in the U.S.A, U.K, U.A.E and China (P.R.C.). He has solid blue-chip corporate experience (Barclays Bank PLC & Ecobank Transnational Inc.) and is also an expert in Islamic Sharia-Compliant financing.

Laban has attained some of the highest accolades in achieving and surpassing sales targets in Banking & Offshore Property sales. He has a special passion in assisting and mentoring individuals tap into their full potential to transform them into high performers, which consequently has merited him the admiration of honest detractors and withstood the betrayal by untrue friends. It hasn't been a surprise. The teachings of this book go far beyond faith and elimination of fears. Secret fears can torment your lives, paralyze and become a hindrance to reaching your peak performance. Most sales people are gripped by this inner fear manifested in procrastinating to call and schedule appointments with prospects.

This book also reveals the truth associated with being self-disciplined which is a magnet to success and all what God destined for you. It entails doing what you are supposed to do whether you like or not and without the need of someone telling you what needs to be done in order to achieve success in sales and eventually attaining your life goals and revel about it.

"Laban writes very fluidly with an easy to assimilate methodology. This book should revolutionize your sales approach and subsequently, your results..."

-Mwaniki Mageria
 RiverWood Filmmaker
 Media Personality & Marketing Professional

Acknowledgements

I owe gratitude to the authors before me. Their books are an inspiration and motivation; they have shaped my thoughts and my life – without them, I wouldn't be who I am today.

Dedication

To My late Mother, Isabella Wangui Toni, My best friend I ever had in this world. Her love and devotion was 32 standard squared deviations above the mean. This book is to you, for what you taught me has become my daily mantra.

Foreword

The most important ideas about reading this wonderful book is the ability to understand and tap deeply into the five Secrets of Selling and Marketing via the ADVCA processes namely; 'The Power of Attraction, Differentiation, Visibility, Credibility, and Authority' towards achieving your sales targets and surpassing your expectations.

Laban clearly outlines that the pillars of selling in a globalized, digitized, and fast paced economy requires bold moves which are enshrined and come from understanding the terrain and mastery of the five Secrets of Selling.

I highly recommend you to read and appreciate the simple and yet authoritative processes he covers in this intense book on selling and marketing if you want to transform your career as well as your company and generally the quality of your life. As for those who are in senior sales and marketing jobs the book is a must read and will introduce you to new concepts and techniques that have been proven globally. The book also forms a good read for those who want to understand the power of the African Global Diaspora economy, and its purchasing power.

By Dr. Ali Abdullahi, **Ph.D**
CEO, Amsas Consulting Pty. Ltd., Sydney, Australia

Introduction

Having experienced some of the bottlenecks in closing a variety of sales from products to services, I could not hesitate to put together a manual that would resolve the nightmare of most salespeople who have to keep changing jobs from company to company, industry to industry to keep up with the sales jobs and the related targets.

This amazing book is not only for those who have just began their journey in a great sales career, but also for the veteran and battle-scarred sales professional seeking to refine as well as upscale their expertise in sales. It is a guideline on how to achieve excellence in sales as well as sales management that will translate into a great sales career, potentially improving income earning ability in terms of upfront commissions, reputation and prestige that comes along with it. Businesses will nonetheless, flourish and enjoy increased volumes of sales as well as improve their bottom line, PBT (profit before tax), pay other bonuses and promote high achievers.

The customers' mindsets have changed over time and therefore it would be prudent to expect that the approach by salespeople would consequently change to keep abreast with the changing tastes and preferences of customers'. Albert Einstein famously proclaimed the definition of insanity as believing that you could keep on *doing what you have been doing*, and still *expect different results*. If you don't change your sales techniques to match the changing mindset of consumers, your sales will definitely be adversely affected without a shadow of doubt.

Many salespeople have negated their own personal influence on the products and services they offer to their customers relying mostly on published materials such as presentations, brochures and flyers. Actually the only time customers have a connection to your product, is when you have personal approval ratings higher than those of the product and/or service that you are offering, followed by the company you represent and that is how it translates into a sale. In essence the customer buys you and not the product per se, and therefore image is everything and therefore your first impression really matters in your sales career.

I will include this piece of inspirational information in this part of the introduction from a sales talk that I first attended at the launch of a network marketing company, Smart Travel in Arlington, TX, U.S.A in 2001. On that evening of the launch, the speaker had introduced more than one hundred new founder members who surprisingly were all introduced into the business model by one, Wayne Newjerk.

This was the first time I had heard of the term Power Seller, and Wayne Newjerk really was one. His outstanding sales performance stood out on that night. He had single handedly approached all the more than one hundred prospects in attendance at the launch and convinced them to join within a fortnight. When he took center stage to give a vote of thanks, he attributed this extra ordinary performance on the power of his credibility. He not only was knowledgeable about the business that he presented to the prospects, but he combined this with enthusiasm, confidence and impeccable mannerism he portrayed along the sales process. This made lasting impressions on his prospects and that was his secret of transmuting prospects into confirmed sales by creating attraction for what he represented. This marked the birth of my sales career and to this date, I have never looked back.

> *"Men and women are limited not by the place of their birth, not by the color of their skin, but by the size of their hope."- John Johnson*

The rationale behind rolling out this self-help book is to generate authoritative sales and create uncontested market space and render the competition irrelevant.

Enjoy this interesting and beneficial read that will make you a power seller. Promoting sales is like setting out on a journey, your journey begins here.

Chapter 1

THE POWER OF ATTRACTION; MAKING THE PROSPECTS COME TO YOU

Congratulations, You're about to graduate with a Ph.D. of Selling!

For those who have the notion that generation of sales revenue is meant for salespeople, reflect again! We all engage in the art of generating sales at one point or another. **Generating of sales** is an attribute of all prosperous people. It's therefore imperative to note that this is the one-on-one process of sharing valuable information leading up to a sale which doesn't have to be work related. This book goes beyond sales and is also for anyone adding value to this society to change its landscape and live it a better world than you found it.

A good example is when you work on a project. You will have to make decisions on how the project will run or more intricately you will have to trade ideas on how to treat a member who is not a team-player. Similarly when you are out with friends you will have to sell your opinions on what mode of transport to use whether the metro train or take a ride on an Uber or where you want to go out for lunch either at Steak & Ale or do McDonalds. Whether you realize it or not, you exercise the art of selling every day.

If you have been is sales for more than 5 years or longer and your sales results are beginning to plummet, this is a clear indication that a paradigm shift needs to take place. If you are still imploring old sales methods and strategies, it is about time to learn some new sales techniques through a refresher course as the old methods do not work anymore or 2 finite things may happen; *Either*

1) Improve on your sales techniques *Or*
2) Continue experiencing poor sales and face imminent exit from the market place

Changing Mindsets of Customers.

How have customers changed since the 1990s? Are they more skeptical about Salespeople? According to Gerry Robert in his book the *Millionaire's mindset*, there is no shortage of seminars, coaches and books teaching people strategies that neither understand the changes in the consumer's mindset nor the effective methods to produce great sales results.

According to Antony Robbins, the power to magically transfigure our lives into our greatest dreams lies within us all. The purpose of this book is to share with you how to have uncontested share in the marketplace, and make a difference in your life.

In the olden days power was thought of in terms of subduing people. *The king* was seen as the symbol of power and ruled with unmistakable authority. The sycophantic cohorts derived power through their association with the king. This type of power does not last forever and therefore we should be particularly conscious of the actions that those wielding such State Powers take. Then there emerged the industrial age where *capital* was the power. According to me the ultimate power rests with the ability to produce the results you desire and add value to other people's lives along the process. Those who had the means dominated the industrial age and you will agree with me it is better to have capital than it is not to possess it. Today the largest form of power lies in having *specialized knowledge*. I'm sure most of you have heard that we are now living in the modern times and what is referred to as the information age. We are primarily a communication culture and no longer an industrial one. The new world order is stratified with those who have information and therefore the agents of change and those who do not and therefore must function out of ignorance. If we had always been delivered to inaction by our lack of complete information, today we would still be hunters and gatherers on the earth's savannahs. This means that everyone has access to this form of power, unlike in the ancient times where it would have been an uphill task to become a king. Now there is unlimited access to specialized knowledge that can transform this world. It can be accessed from libraries, bookshops, seminars, workshops, online search engines, YouTube and other social media platforms. The list is endless. With access to this sort of information there are people who are generating great results while others are just still wallowing with dismal results and apportioning blame on others. Why aren't they, happy, wealthy, prosperous, wise and downright successful? The answer lies with taking action. *Power is described as the ability to act*, while *knowledge has been known to be potential power*. Until such a time that you decide to put the specialized knowledge into action is when your world transfigures. Action is what unites success.

The gift that most successful people have over the average man is their ability to take decisive action. Many people have access to information and opportunities as much as Dr. Chris Kirubi does. But Dr. Chris Kirubi who is a business mogul in Nairobi and also a member of the Harvard's Africa Advisory Board was able to take action and by doing this he has changed the shopping experience in Nairobi at the Two Rivers Mall.

It is my sincere hope that you will find the skills, strategies and new ways to sell today in the market place from prospecting to following up and even closing a sale revealed within these pages as empowering as they have been for me.

> *"Once your mindset changes, everything on the outside will change along with it."*
> - Steve Maraboli

Sales Rule #1 Forget About What You've Ever Learnt in Sales

First and foremost, I think all what we have learnt over the years on sales is useful to us but we should not be fanatics of what we know – learning is a process- so we keep adding to it. Many salespeople have been trained to manipulate customers and coerce them into buying. This doesn't create a lasting relationship. More often than not antagonizes the relationship between the seller and the new customer once they find about the sales person's insincerity in disclosing all the attributes of a beneficial service or product they are offering.

1. Marketers need to get off the short term selling model and embrace relationships with their customers referred to as the *"marriage-model"* to claim their rightful position in the market place. Many marketers for lack of a proper sales and marketing plan embark on cold calls. The notion is that the more doors you knock will eventually translate into sales. This is actually a myth. One thing that we are not told about this unproductive method is the emotional toll of being rejected 9 out of 10 times. This is also a waste of company's resources from marketing materials like printed brochures and flyers, transport costs and deliberate salespeople's efforts using solid arguments to sell products and services to prospective customers which are not proven to produce meaningful results. No wonder salespeople keep moving from company to company, industry to industry, thinking they would actually get immune to rejection and eventually master the art of being sleek and manipulating prospects into buying.

"Your professionalism is defined not by the business you are in, but by the way you are in business" -Tony Alessandra

Make Them Come Running Directly to You

2. Did you know that it costs five times more to bring on board new customers than it would actually cost to keep and sustain an already existing happy customer? According to Lee Ann Obringer, who is both a designer and an author, her client once explained, "Some of my best experiences with salespeople were with those who honestly listened to my needs, and showed an interest in more than just the business. They came in with a low pressure, open, and honest approach and won my business. I didn't mind setting up appointments for their visits. I looked forward to them. It was low pressure and friendly. My company received good service, good prices, and everyone was happy. I knew they would react quickly if I had problems or emergency needs. So, when competitors called, I quickly told them we were happy with our current vendor - even if they may have been able to give us a better price! That's part of the power of relationship selling!"

    Relationship selling: This is the deliberate act of nurturing a friendship or building rapport with prospects to know of their needs and wants. Upon establishing a relationship, demonstrated you care, and gotten their trust, it's almost a certainty you are on the road-map to making them your esteemed customers. The relationship model treats customers more like long-time partners unlike the archaic methods which seem like a one-night stand where the marketer only concentrates on making a sale and achieving a personal gain. The *"marriage-model,"* where the marketer and client schedule regular service calls, becomes a solutions provider and the client eventually turns to an advocate for the business is very effective in making them run after you.

The way most salespeople sell is similar to a one-night stand. They lie and even make exaggerated claims. They will go to any extent just to make a sale. This is characterized by overpromising and under-delivering. These types of marketers wait for a problem to develop and always wait for customers to call them and are quick to blame somebody else if things go wrong. The marriage model is where the money is. The winners today adopt the marriage model.

It's no wonder that the highest income earners and power sellers are not using outdated methods of making cold calls and subjecting prospects and customers to manipulation.

The relationship or marriage model has 4 elaborate steps;

i. First it's the manner of approach which encompasses building trust and establishing a rapport.
ii. The second step is conducting the need analysis through probes, asking the prospect questions and listening very carefully to establish possible opportunities. For example, the marital status of the prospect can indicate whether to follow up for additional sales for the spouse and/or children. These are usually lost opportunities for marketers using old methods of selling as they will only focus on the sale at hand with no intention of establishing a long term relationship.
iii. The third stage is making the presentation. This is where the marketer sells the benefits to the client. In traditional selling the marketer will only present the product features and hasten the sales process to closing long and hard and all the benefits of a relationship disregarded and lost forever.
iv. The last step in the relationship/marriage model involves gaining commitment and managing resistance, reassuring and finally ending up in closing the sale.

This model wins the day and keeps the customers coming and makes them have no reason to be looking elsewhere as they are rest assured of the best prices, deals and bargains. Marketers using the traditional model loose allegiance of their customers to them and therefore customers and treat them as statistics. The marriage model differs very much in its approach as clients are treated as entities and specifics are used to heighten their satisfaction levels. Treat customers like you treat your paycheck or salary check. When you loose your good clients, you have no one to pay you! Treat them like they are your boss. Here are some of the simple specifics to extend to your customers

1. Give sincere gratitude to customers for channeling their business to you.
2. Make it a norm to go an extra-mile to please your customers.
3. Learn to impress your customers, as though you're seeking for a pay rise
4. Every time you converse with your customer, think of your paycheck
5. Maintain your integrity and keep promises

"It's not enough to love your product. You have to love your customers too, every single one—those who complain the most are the ones who control the keys to your survival."
- Ken Goldstein

3. Another way to keep the customers running after you is by recognizing them by name. Clients are served on an individual basis with TLC (tender loving care) unlike in traditional sales methods where customers are served as part of the mass. Remember the last time you went to a restaurant and called the waiter by their name which you had just read from their name tag, did you notice how the waiter responded affirmatively with a friendly and personalized service? This has the same effect when you know most of the 20% of your clients who

mostly end up generating 80% of your revenue. When a client has been featured in the local dailies or newspaper, pick up the phone and call to congratulate them or have the newspaper cutting affixed on the public notice board if this doesn't violate your company policies. This is also referred to as **consultative selling** or **customer intimacy**

"Nobody will listen to you unless they sense that you like them."
- Donald Miller

Consultative selling involves positioning yourself as a friend and consultant to your customers. It involves a salesperson presenting themselves as a specialist consultant who probes the customer to establish their needs and wants and offers them the best solution which will be more beneficial to the client. This involves strategically placing yourself before the customer as an expert in an effort that will influence the customers' perception to choose their product and brand relative to other competing products or brands.

The Secret is Attraction!

4. Another effective method of making customers run after you is by embracing the 90 days on boarding cycle. This means that when a customer decides to buy your product or use your service, they are actually in switch mode and need to be engaged or else they could switch elsewhere. This is because of increased competition from new entrants and established players; consumers are quite informed with abilities to search online, product commoditization as modifications can be replicated in no time.

The moment a customer decides to purchase a product, an invisible clock begins to tick. It's therefore critical that, within these 90 days' period you engage clients by calling them to collect their Automated

Teller Machine (ATM) cards, check books as and when they are received, notify them of a possible service interruption, delay in services such as cheque (check) book requests not being received on time etc. Fact-finding has revealed repeatedly that after the clock ticks for 90 days, a period referred to as *"on boarding"* – this essentially means the customer's profitability and lifetime value would have been determined and cast on stone. This creates trust and lasting relationships and the customer keeps coming back.

5. Today, financial institutions and many other businesses are uncovering other means of conducting the process of on boarding to enhance lifetime value, increase cross-selling, optimize profits and inspire customer loyalty. Most people are *multi-banked* meaning they have more than one bank account. When a customer is made to feel important, this creates attraction and makes them come to you and this also creates an opportunity to request them to increase their wallet share and channel most of their banking and business through you. At this point where the customer is satisfied with your services, it creates the right opportunity to seek at least 5 referrals from them and this will further translate into greater sales since the customer has been turned into a partner and can advocate products and services you are offering to his family, relatives, friends and colleagues. This is also called **Partnering for profits approach**. To differentiate yourselves from other salespeople, it's important to market position yourself like a business partner, continually searching for ways to make-better or enhance the customers' business.

Revamp Your Customer's Commercial Activities

You can be rest assured, dealings with a business person will reveal the thing they think about perpetually is always their business. It is dear to their heart and very close to them. If you visit their business premises, talk as well as find out how their business is doing, share improved processes to help their business run better, the customer will loosen up and get ready to have a business relationship with you and your company.

The Business Expansion Model

6. According to Zig Ziglar in his book *You can reach the top,* an Italian engineer, socialist, scientist, economist and philosopher came up with the "80/20 rule" way back in the 1990's. His theory stated that, in many businesses, 20% of the products represented 80% of the income. It's therefore widely accepted that a small percentage of the population will give a greater portion of the sales volume. It's fair therefore to assume that the 20% represents the known customers who have already done business or will purchase your product or use your service within the next weeks, months or years.

The other 80% comprises of the unbanked population or the unknown market and is the composition of the large majority out there and where most businesses try to establish sales from. It is no wonder that some salespeople work very hard yet they produce dismal results. It's because they concentrate on the population which is most unlikely to make a purchase that will translate into a sale.

The winners only concentrate on the 20% who are more predisposed to buying your product and services and that will yield 80% of your income. This is the segment that salespeople need to concentrate their efforts, time and money on.

> *"The goal of many leaders is to get people to think more highly of the leader. The goal of a great leader is to help people think more highly of themselves." - John Maxwell*

7. According to Zig Ziglar, in an organization with an average of 100 employees, almost 8 employees do not fit in at all, 6

out of the 100 employees will be high performers with 8 times more production per employee as the rest of the 86 remaining employees. This high productivity is as a direct result of their attitudes, what they engage in and overall how they relate with other people. The high performers thrive on these three major components – *product knowledge, skills set and attitude*. A lot of salespeople are culpable of concentrating most of their time and energy on – product knowledge and skills set, and leave out the most important ingredient and attribute, inculcation of an upright attitude. These three, all lubricate the gearwheels of a high sales performer; however attitude is considered the top most oil grade.

The question ringing in your mind now is, "why don't companies hire more high-performers?" The answer is you can't hire them, you have to develop them. According to Forbes magazine most managers hire someone "safer" than a super-smart and outspoken firebrand. They hire someone more pliable, who will do what they're told to do without complaining. They get the workforce trained as a sign of showing they are an asset to the company, increase their loyalty and reduce staff turnover. Retention is always a big cost saving to most companies. The high-performers work in the corporate world for a little while and then step out to be on their own. They want to call the shots in their business life, and in their career.

Some companies are of the notion, "why should we train our people then loose them?" Obviously the response would be; "One thing worse than training people and losing them, is not training them and keeping them."

8. **Sales Efficiency vs. Sales Effectiveness**

In any business model offering products and services at a price, there is one fact that is unique to all; without an efficient sales process, regardless of how great your products and services are, the business is predestined to struggle if it fails to appeal and attract customers.

9. The primary focus of sales systems has been creating efficiency of the salesperson and the sales management process. The only downside is they have not been able to assist people to be better in selling. They have failed to provide tools that salespeople need to bring deals to fruition. Is it prudent to maintain *efficiency* as the focal point in sales, or would it be time to shift focus to *effectiveness*?

But just how different is sales efficiency from sales effectiveness?

Sales Efficiency is a product of the volume of tasks we perform correctly. Efficiency increases every time we apply processes and tools to speed up or when we save time by cutting unnecessary steps.

Sales Effectiveness is a product of the outcome we get. Effectiveness in sales in any organization comes from up scaling the ways the sales team operates. Through sharing and applying industry best-practices, incorporating ways with capabilities to gauge performance, drastically reducing deal closure cycles, and tremendously improving on the percentage of business you win.

It's pretty obvious here that to attract customers and close more deals, you will need to be effective. I shall be taking you through ways to be effective to attract more and more customers by doing more of these very simple things yet overlooked to keep the customers coming.

> *Efficiency is doing things right. Effectiveness is doing the right thing*
> *- Thomas K. Connellan*

10. **Things typical salespeople do, that you shouldn't do.**

i. The stereotypical salesman is pushy. Pushy refers to pressure emanating from external stimuli and exerting itself on a prospect. The pressure is not inward and it's evidently outwardly imposed upon. There's pressure that is not coming from the interior, its coming from the exterior. It's saying, "You should get in, you should do this". Do the contrary, be a pulley. Cross-examine with questions like, "Why did you agree to this meeting? What were you hoping to gain? What in your life are you hoping to change maybe? Maybe I may help you out?" That's pulling. This is the art of pulling information and intent out of a prospect. It's internal based. Pulling, you're not going to get resistance. The average salesman enjoys doing all the talking. Don't fall in that trap, do the reverse, Listen instead. By listening, prospects will confide in you about characteristics they have issues with and find unpleasant, objectionable and off-putting in typical salespeople. Prospects like to carryout business with admirable salespeople with customary traits like ability to listen, results oriented, modesty, curiosity, and not easily discouraged or intimidated. Reflect on the type of salesperson you would want to buy from, and adopt that pleasant personality in your sales.

   "I'll give you money to buy what I'm selling, because I'm a savvy salesman."
   - Jarod Kintz

ii. **The Power of Selling With a Smile**
   The primary goal of any sales person when working with a new potential client is to get them to like you. Successful salespeople looking to instantly develop rapport with a new customer know the importance of a smile. One obvious but sometimes overlooked tip to establish rapport in an instant is: *Offer up a Smile.* Surprisingly, research has proved we're actually born

smiling. When we are happy, the natural response is to smile. Smiling takes no skill to do it, or undergo any form of training, and it actually increases your face value. Research conducted by Tara Kraft and Sarah Pressman known as the Clever Study, revealed that even forcing or faking a smile can make you happier as well as reduce your levels of stress.

According to Forbes Magazine, by measuring the smiles in the photographs of students taken in a year book, researchers were able to predict: how satisfied they would be in their marriages as well as how long they would last, level of scores they would attain on standardized tests of generally living happily and offering inspiration to others. A straight-forward reaction of smiling offers the most powerful ways to get over unfortunate circumstances, disputes and failures. If a contract or deal has fizzled out or fallen through, the first reaction to counter negativity is a *smile*. A smile projects positivity and pulls in people instantly as it is an affirmative reciprocation to life situations.

"If you're reading this...Congratulations, you're alive. If that's not something to smile about, then I don't know what is." – Chad Sugg

iii. **Be a Real Person by** displaying the great qualities of the person you are by sharing stories, dreams and ambitions with your prospective clients. This act in itself will demonstrate that you are a fascinating, enthusiastic and energetic person who is working their way up to be a well-to-do and prosperous person. This will create good feelings of customers and prospects purchasing from you, because apart from receiving great service, they in essence know they are helping a good person climb up the ladder of success and in achieving their ambitions.

"Impression, not oppression determines the real life of a real person." - Israelmore Ayivor

iv. **Really Listen.** Sales skill number#1 is *listening*. By design we were created with two ears and a single mouth which symbolizes that we need to concentrate on listening, twice more than we talk. By really listening, it conveys the message that you are a kind-hearted, thoughtful and a diplomatic person. Be focused more on the sense of hearing than what comes out of your mouth. You need to demonstrate to your prospect or customer and show you are really listening. How can you do this? By using summary statements to establish you have heard, using queries to clarify, and using body language to show that you are really listening. If you pay attention by listening to your customer, they share with you what their needs are. While on the other hand, if you spend more time talking, you are in essence creating more time and ways for the customer or prospects to say, "NO".

"When people talk, listen completely. Most people never listen." -Ernest Hemingway

v. **Being Vulnerable** is one of the techniques that builds rapport in an instant yet it's the least discussed and a very important attribute of a successful salesperson. By sharing our fears and disappointments with customers and prospects, usually the notion is; we could be opening ourselves to getting hurt, as a result few people practice it. Our concern is how people will become cognizant of this fact and we try to do everything possible to safeguard our self-image. Actually when we become vulnerable, we share human qualities. Sharing vulnerability is usually the start of an open and genuine relationship. Vulnerability is a solid tool to build relationships; however, it MUST be used with sincerity. If we are sincere and have a great personality and perceive our responsibility as providing service to our customers we have nothing to worry about by sharing our inner feelings, as a matter of fact we have everything to benefit from. However, if you use this mechanism to benefit in terms of influence, power, position and money through manipulation of customers, the result can be disastrous. People will read you like a book. The reason behind this is that your success radiates from your personality and character, and not from the words you cautiously choose and utter or the script you rehearse from.

"What happens when people open their hearts?" "They get better." - Haruki Murakami

vi. **Dress professionally.** According to Lillian D. Bjorseth to be successful the personal experience begins the very moment someone gets a glimpse of you…even before uttering a word. It's important that the encounter begins on the right vein and therefore why you should portray a proper persona both in ways of behaving and outward look. First impressions can become a self-fulfilling prophecy and could influence your interactions as well as opportunities, since people decide 10 things relating to you within 10 seconds of meeting you. Business has never been casual, clients and prospects appreciate dealings with salespeople who look prosperous. Walk in a law firm, and you won't be able to tell the difference in the professional attire between a pupil and a senior advocate. The same can be said of doctors and bankers who are well-to-do professionals being paid to provide advice and counsel. Therefore it's important that your clothes be highly-priced, smart, neat and orderly. The hair should look humbly done, hands clean and fingers well-manicured. When your outlook is good, chances are an even better feeling will emanate from the inside. Feeling good has the effect of always keeping you at peak performance without having to worry about anything.

"You can't climb the ladder of success, dressed in the costume of failure." - Zig Ziglar

vii. **Learn from con artists**
When people like you they will have a reason to listen to you, and when people trust you they will want to do business with you. Though most people perceive con men as sweet talkers, they actually practice and apply rapport building techniques. Psychological research has shown that they actually bond with their victims through listening. Chris Voss, a former FBI hostage negotiator also revealed they make use of this method of really listening to build rapport between captor(s) and hostages. Often aired are tales of outlandish fraudulent schemes on television and newspapers. The commonality of the victims' narratives is always they, "liked and trusted" the con men. Rapport building tactics are centered on *like and trust*. The con artists are portrayed at work through hidden cameras extracts. How successful would the con artists been had they been legitimately pushing products and services? Learn from the con artists and implement some of these techniques of rapport building to improve and upscale your personal sales career.

"Selling eternal life is an unbeatable business, with no customers ever asking for their money back after the goods are not delivered." – Victor J. Stenger

viii. **Fighting Competition, an exercise in Futility.**
When a customer has previously bought from the competition, they must have had a valid reason for exercising that choice. If you query such a purchase decision, you are in other words questioning the customer's choice or at least suggesting they have poor judgment or taste. Probe to find out the needs the competitor brand falls short of satisfying. Thereafter, follow it

up with attributes of your product and service that will fill in the missing gaps of the competitor's product and service without denigrating their product or service.

ix. **Leave Sincere and Specific Compliments**
Truth be said, there is immense power and profound effect that a sincere compliment has on someone. Compliments can possibly permeate throughout that person's life.

"Pay with compliments and you will always be wealthy."
~Mike Dolan

Is it hard for you to sincerely compliment a random stranger or even someone you know? Yes it is, but the compliment need be sincere and secondly it has to address specifics. For example if you admire somebody's automobile, the make, house, office, the garden, the front lounge, the furnishings, paintings etc. be sure to mention out the specifics.

"You cannot receive a sincere compliment without feeling better...and just as important, you cannot give a sincere compliment without feeling better yourself!"

Chapter 2

THE POWER OF DIFFERENTIATION; SETTING YOU APART FROM OTHER SALES PEOPLE

The general market place is not able to tell the difference between you and other salespeople in the competition. In the mind of today's customer, you are just one and the same as any other salespeople despite your specialized training and the fact that you provide satisfaction to your customers. This means that despite your efforts to have signage on office doors, advertise on the Daily Nation, The East African Standard, The Tampa tribune, Dallas Morning News, Daily News, New York Times, Yellow pages, distribute colorful flyers, brochures and leaflets bearing elaborate company logos, the market place still does not recognize you are different from the rest and they think you all bear similarities.

This sameness occurs as a result of habit when people emulate what the others are doing without putting much thought into it. The resultant effect can be disastrous, unless significant steps are taken to remedy this situation and resolve it permanently. The solution lies in differentiation, which is the promotional method employed by a business or sales person to create a strong presence, create leverage and set you apart from the rest in a particular market.

The competition out there is real and unless you find a way to differentiate yourself from other salespeople and establish your identity in a crowded market place, you are doomed for poor sales results.

Differentiation Approaches that Work

1. **The greeters program** is a way of showing hospitality and welcoming customers and visitors to your place of business. This program is well executed when a member of management carries it out. Envision the branch manager welcoming you personally to the business premises, opening the doors and asking you what brings you to the business premises.

   I personally used this approach at an Islamic financial institution, when I was appointed as the Regional Manager in charge of Corporate and Institutional banking for the Coastal region at their Mombasa Branch, Kenya in 2014. I spent an hour between 9-10:00 am every Wednesday morning, welcoming my esteemed customers to the Bank. I went further to maintain a log of what brought the customers to the Bank and tracked the progress in order to favour the customers with a response on their specific requests. The rewards were most gratifying and deeply personal. The customers were magnetized to the service and in turn we took this opportunity upon ourselves to request them to transact more with us. This resulted in more business and increase in their wallet share.

   This had the effect of turning them into loyal customers and I therefore found it very easy to rally their support behind me and keeping in tandem with the Bank's mission and vision of growth. I tried to meet my targets within my 3 months stipulated probation period. With this effective approach, I was able to not only achieve but also exceed my branch annual deposit target within three months.

2. **Do Prospects see You any Differently than any of the Competitors?**
   One-Stop-Shop strategy - Customers look for value, not the circles or chains behind it. Do you create and deliver value as close as possible to the customer? An effective way to present value solutions to a customer is through the One-Stop-Shop strategy. 'One-Stop-Shop' is whereby you supply ALL of your products or services, with ONE invoice, ONE delivery and you deal with ONE point of contact.

   Not only does this help to simplify your supply chain, it offers you a selective and specialized personal service. In this information technology edge, for example an ICT firm that offers a client technology assessment, system integration, staffing, contract negotiations, technology sourcing and post implementation maintenance under one roof is more preferable and stands out.

   It follows that it provides superior customer experience since most of the needs and requirements of the client are addressed at the same time and the customer needs to look no further for alternative solution providers. The One-Stop-Shop strategy can be achieved through a network and resource pool by enhancing customer experiences through strong business alliances, industry contacts, resources with technology companies, sourcing partners and service providers.

3. **Tailor-Made Solutions**. Another great approach is to tailor make solutions for your customers. Many salespeople give the prescription of one size fits all. This has the effect of giving a much generalized approach and solutions.

   "You will make an appalling somebody else, as you're the best "you" existing. You are the only unique person who can utilize your capability. It's an awesome responsibility"

The sales person that goes out of their way to get tailor-made solutions for customers wins the day. Customers' look for value and the way you do business to grow, attract and keep profitable customers will need to keep changing over time. The strategy is to differentiate yourself from your competitors in ways that the target audiences will value. For instance, a company may contact you for business, but ask for preferential pricing.

Most salespeople shy away from making any efforts to get better pricing for their customers as they are motivated to only achieve their sales targets, this drives them away to competition. When such an opportunity presents itself, it's prudent to go an extra mile to understand the customers' business. It's also a great chance to negotiate for more business in order to justify for the preferential pricing request.

Your attitude determines (establishes) your altitude, as you cannot go higher than you think you can.

This is a great strategy and creates a win-win situation in that you are able to book more business from a single customer and they in return enjoy negotiated rates.

4. **Show Gratitude: Experience a Better Life Instantly**. Striving to show gratitude to your customers is a great thing to do; however, words don't bear the intensity and profundity of actions. If you offer valuable customer service, in one way or the other, it's important to consistently express gratitude in exciting, pleasing and unforgettable ways.

"As we express our gratitude, we must never forget that the highest appreciation is not to utter words, but to live by them – John F. Kennedy"

It's important to ensure that all efforts geared towards expressing gratitude to customers are utmost sincere, noticeable, personalized and relevant. When crafting thank you notes to your customers, it's important to be more specific and focused. Rather than just saying, "Thank you for your business;" it would be quite effective to say something like, "Thank you for being our partner, working with your dedicated company has taught me the importance of communicating proactively and staying accountable throughout the process." These simple requirements will ensure your show of hits home with customers. Stories of amazing customer service overtures fill the air - it's time to let your company be the story of the day.

I used this strategy at an Islamic financial institution when I acted as the Area Manager for the Mombasa branches in Kenya from October –December 2013. Customers love the red carpet treatment, which is why I chose it to use it on selected days to *WOW* them to a treat of two different blends of coffee and niceties such as cookies and dates served within the vicinity of the bank. The customer service experience was delightfully over-the-top that the customers had a great story to tell and before long this strategy was adopted across the Bank and dubbed *Marhaba* day.

It was not just a fun moment for the customers; I also took it upon myself to ensure it was another interactive forum with a delighted customer to cross-sell to. This platform proved to be useful and we took it upon ourselves to drum for more business for other bank products and alternative channels such as mobile banking, savings accounts for children and spouse, agency banking, order for ATM cards etc., and this had the effect of improving the bank's revenue lines.

5. **Role Playing for Success**. If you want your staff to offer hats off consumer interaction, look no further! This is the deliberate

act of members of senior management usually sitting at the Head Offices to attend to and serve the customers at the branch level. For example, the Treasurer serving clients as a cashier (teller). They would usually perform roles such as those at the customer service desk, cashier (teller); receiving and paying out cash.

Below herein are well-suited examples for Role-Playing:

- Problem analysis on different aspects' e.g. customer service, maintenance department, back office, sales department etc.
- Build partnership, teamwork, cooperation as well as innovative trouble-shooting in cross-functional groups.
- Develop rapport with customers and increase confidence of the customers and make them feel they are appreciated and can easily interact with senior members of management.

Chapter 3

THE POWER OF VISIBILTY; HAVING MORE OF THE RIGHT PEOPLE IN FRONT OF YOU

Selling a great idea for a revolutionary product or a better way to perform an everyday task within your company requires support from the right people. Unless you have a close personal relationship with someone who can turn your idea into reality, it's an important attribute to swiftly get more of the right people in front of you. Calling every person who might possibly be interested in your idea could get results, but more likely will lead to nothing but frustration because getting people's attention is ever more difficult and you could end up with a huge phone bill. Instead, develop a targeted plan to meet the important decision makers and you will be on your way to a great selling career.

In *Think and Grow Rich* by Napoleon Hill, he found out that each of the 500 millionaires interviewed for the book, in fact, had their main goals written on a goal card. Even if you don't know how to achieve your sales goal at this point, it's important to still have them written down. Countless thousands of people who have used this relatively simple technique can easily attest to its success.

> *"Important: Until you commit your goals to paper you have intentions that are seeds without soil"*

How to Get in Front of the Right People to Sell

1. Prepare an "elevator speech" of a minute or less that will pique your audience's interest and entice them to help you. The pitch should be simple, memorable, demonstrate the benefits of your product, service or idea, show how it's different than other ideas, and end with a call to action such as a request for a meeting to discuss it in more detail. Research the people who may be most receptive to your idea by examining corporate websites, industry publications, annual reports, popular business publications and news stories about the people you are targeting. Learn about their companies, backgrounds, interests and ideas that they previously supported.
2. Build relationships with people who are at a slightly higher level than you on the corporate ladder. They could possibly introduce you to the right people and also provide backup support for your product, service or idea. Join your company's mentoring program, try and talk to people in the elevator, attend corporate and industry events where you can be able to know people in other departments and companies on a personal level.

Look through the company's website for contact information and contact the CEO or decision-maker directly. Sometimes the CEO's e-mail address is not listed; you should be able to find a means to contact him, through the personal assistants (PA's) office, a "Contact Us" link or by contacting another executive or senior manager.

Ask friends, colleagues and family for introductions and referrals to anyone who they know who may be interested in your idea, product and/or service or who may be able to introduce you to the right people. If you meet with someone who turns down your idea, ask for a referral to someone they know who can help. Attend industry events to meet the decision-makers you need to meet and use your short pitch to ask them for a meeting. Look for them at networking meetings, corporate events and launches, press events as well as conferences. Craft a solid pitch letter, based on your elevator speech, to build interest in your idea and send letters to the people you need to talk with to request for a meeting. Call the people who received your e-mails as follow-up and request for a meeting. You will likely encounter gatekeepers, such as receptionists and assistants, but be consistent and persistent.

> *"How you perceive yourself today will exert influence on how you perform today."*

3. Lack of sales planning and failures in forecasting happen to be the main source of absence of visibility within the sales function of any organization. This can be equated to driving down a winding road without headlights. The absence of visibility is caused by unavailability of critical data to measure and drive sales performance. Envisage a situation where you could easily and automatically get meaningful reports at a touch of a button, which comprehensively shows all key performance indicators (KPI's) on sales; pin points with precision the focal points to refine in order to boost the salespeople's performances.

In order to gain visibility, you first need to understand the metrics that drive sales achievement. The adoption of performance dash boards in organizations has proved to be a useful tool in providing visibility and in developing sales growth plans and forecasts. Some of the guiding indicators to appear on performance dash boards include but are not limited to; the number of sales reps, average production by a sales rep, monthly sales in month 1, 2, 3 and volume and values of sales generated.

> *"Outstanding people share one commonality; an outright cognizance of purpose and/or an absolute sense of mission."*

The reason why organizations transition from good to great is because of the enhanced visibility approach used and the visual tools that help minimize work in progress (W.I.P.) and track development, concluding that visibility within an organization surely leads to success.

Organizations have adopted visual dash boards that monitor performance of their salespeople on a daily basis. For simplicity purposes, this takes the form of the usual notice board but updated with the names of all staff and their daily contribution to the sales of the organization. The targets are usually broken down in yearly amounts but it's prudent to break it further into half-yearly, quarterly, monthly, bi-weekly, weekly and daily for purposes of monitoring.

A typical start of a sales day would be; salespeople assemble at exactly 7:30am and deliberate on challenges faced in the field the previous day and share accomplishments and failures. This would be followed by role playing on how to overcome objections they encountered from prospects and customers. It makes it easier to take remedial action on salespeople who haven't met their weekly targets since the dash boards give early indication of who may after all struggle with their monthly targets or not meet them all together.

I was instrumental in implementing performance dash boards at Barclays Bank PLC, Lead Generator Team (LGT), Digo Road, Mombasa, Kenya in 2009. I updated all the variables on liability and assets products and this gave clear guidelines to the Area Sales Manager on the path the sales department was taking on a daily basis at a quick glance. This visibility of numbers displayed on dash boards creates a more efficient approach to monitor and supervise the sales function and its performance more closely.

It provides a uniform and consolidated plan of action which provides one; combined eyeshot of the salespeople's pipeline with improved visibility as well as abilities to contrast budgeted against the actual sales figures. This makes sales prediction more precise, error-free and a bit more authoritative. Administration of sales targets becomes more efficient, from resource allocation to each sales lead, to supervision of the performance of the sales team against budget/targets. Goal setting for every salesperson according to their budgets and the sales income also raises their accountability. In essence we shape the future when the visibility tool is well implemented and the outcomes are anchored in our minds.

The absence of visibility in the sales teams is a constant weakness and the cause of falling through. It is an issue of concern for the following reasons;

i). Salespeople fail to comprehend their responsibilities in the absence of everyday visibility on the overall performance.
ii). Lack of a visible presentation tool makes it difficult for salespeople to know priority of their duties especially if they are supporting multiple products or services.
iii). Salespeople may also fail to factor in the importance of completing their responsibilities and the targeted results and the advantages to the organization.

Organizations can elude these potential threats such as unmanaged risks, miscommunications, budget overruns and failure to collaborate on key deliverables through visual performance aids, adopt cooperation, and enhanced communication.

4. What is the best way to enhance your visibility, create a sphere of influence, create a name and establish a relationship with clients or prospects? How is communication of who you are and what key-message is conveyed in a manner that will have permanent influence and long-term sales afterlife? The solution is found in something fundamental that was in existence before the present day information age –publishing a book

Gerry Robert in his book the *Millionaire's mindset* depicts the classic example of Dr. Cynthia Barnett on enhancing her power of visibility. She was an executive coach in Norwalk, Connecticut. Having understood the need to gain visibility to improve herself in her profession, she authored a simple 110 page book.

The amazing results were that she received lots of free publicity before the book went to the press. As an author, she was interviewed and used that exposure to even get more interviews. Time Magazine went ahead to feature her in an article about women in transition. A book guarantees you instant and never ending visibility.

Christianity has spread to its present-day magnitude, would this have been possible in the absence of the Bible as its pillar? The same can be said about Islam and the Quran. It's easier to share around Christian doctrines on the faith and beliefs in the form of a book, which without would have been quite strenuous. The foundation of any serious movement or group is deep-rooted in a book and this fact holds true to present day.

Prolific writers who also engage in motivational speaking in a big way such as Anthony Robbins and Jack Canfield rely on frequent book releases to keep on expanding their foothold. Celebrities in the world of entertainment, sports and politics have made it a norm to always churn out a book to bolster their brands, public acknowledgement of their contributor role and notably in the absence of the press who have the tendency to disgrace and put things in bad light. When social media wasn't in existence, books represented the earliest form and took up that space. Anything that begins a discussion and builds a relation is considered social media. Books have prompted innumerable hours of dialogue and in exchange have established relationships amongst authors and readers and even in this day and age books continue to play this role. This is the very reason, why scores of people still take part in social book forums all over the globe. Oprah Winfrey's own very popular book club, opened doors way back in 1996. It selected new fiction books for review that viewers would deliberate upon every month. Owing to the prominence of the book club, many obscure book titles entered the race of best-sellers and turned brand leaders, tremendously up scaling the sales by millions of copies. Along with the Oprah Winfrey Show, the club ended its 15-year run, on May 25, 2011 having recommended 70 books during its 15 years stint.

Authors are usually considered distinctive and intelligent. Writing is laborious, takes diligence and conscientious efforts to complete and draws feelings akin to finishing leftover Math assignment in early school. Exactly the reason why most people wouldn't dare to write a book and anybody who completes one is instantaneously held in high esteem, adulation and recognition even without publishing it.

A book bolsters your brand. It becomes excruciatingly difficult to address an audience when there is chitter-chatter going on updating of status on Instagram and Facebook on cellular phones and tablets. With a book you have the opportune time to have their attention, fully engaging the reader in whatever discussion you choose. It provides an excellent window of opportunity to tailor your communiqué and ensure it is conveyed uninterrupted. When one scrutinizes your book, you delve into their cranium for hours on end and this presents a good time to make your point in an expressive and meaningful way. This is also a great moment since there is no one to settle cores or disputes with; it's just you the writer and the reader. This is no longer a one-pager, a book is a complete revelation of how stuff works and this gives you a perfect platform for that. This guarantees respect, admiration and immediate reverence.

You may think to yourself…who has that spare time to read anymore? Especially in this information age when everyone is chit-chatting on their iPhones, watching movies on their iPods, playing videos, fun games and listening to recorded stuff on iPods or viewing podcasts or whichever way they please to pass their leisure time.

We have come to the best part. *Regardless of whether your book is read or not*, the book was the initial reason for the discussion with people. It's neither the beginning nor the end, but certainly it opens the doors for genuine, unparalleled and exceptional marketing opportunities. Brian Tracy a known media celebrity is reputed as one who understands the worth of a book. Every so often he releases a book twice or even thrice annually. This he doesn't do for financial gain, but certainly Brian Tracy knows what to do with a book. His main business is motivational public speaking and he is also a self-development author, but Brian Tracy is good in marketing the brand Brian Tracy – he utilizes his books as a forum for that purpose.

It's All About Customer Experience (CX)

5. A customer-centric company is one that offers more than just good service. It's a priority for such a company to provide first-class and outstanding customer service experience from the point-of-sale and post-sales in a bid to increase profits as well as gaining a competitive edge. A customer-centric organization takes effort to identify the most valued customers and also ensure their satisfaction through availing relevant offers at the opportune time to them. The mindset in that organization is such that all the stakeholders contribute towards enhancing the customer service experience for the most profitable customers' i.e. customers with high lifetime value. These are considered the high net worth clients(HNW) and companies who concentrate their marketing efforts on this customer segment to drive their key performance indicators(KPI's) such as *sales and profits* and also offer them exceptional customer service experience are considered **customer-centric organizations.** All the functional departments such as administration, finance and accounts, human resources, sales and marketing, distribution etc. all work towards a magnificent customer service experience.

Have you called a company and while waiting to speak to a customer service representative they play a recorded message like, *"Your call is important to us. Please stay on the line for the next available representative"*? Being kept on hold and hearing such a recorded message hardly makes you feel you are important to the company. Such companies aren't considered to be customer-centric because listening to such a recorded message rarely makes you feel like the most valued customer and how much you are worth to them.

Dr. Fred Fader who has written extensively on "customer-centrism" shared his sentiments. He expressed the fact that most companies that are dominant market players don't even know their most valued customers who also happen to contribute significantly towards their revenue and profits generation.

Internet: Transforming How You Engage Your Customers:

6. Organizations are looking into ways to enhance their customer service experience.

Pleasing and enchanting customers in this day and age entails 2 things:

a) Identifying and nurturing relationships with customers
b) Capability to provide a harmonious customer service experience covering all the functional departments

Internet is revolutionizing how sales are being conducted today. Apart from extending the bandwidth of clients that are accessible across the globe, it also provides a gateway to products, services and information like never before.

With the explosion of internet in the late 20th Century, predictions were rife that, sales forces across the world would become extinct. With the advent of internet, roles have either been eliminated or automated. Websites like Travelocity, Trip Advisor, and Booking.com have automated the roles of travel agents and you can virtually make online flight bookings and obtain hotel reservations as well as travel plans. Nevertheless, Internet being an enemy of the salespeople seems to have been a grotesque misconception. As a matter of fact, it has become the salespeople's "best friend". The notion was that internet would replace salespeople; it has instead made them even more powerful with tools such as the Internet-enabled CRM. This has made salespeople to be able to even sell more effectively and in an efficient way in any corner of the globe.

Another way is by the organization being 360-degrees visible. This delivers a number of tools that assist to supervise the process of 2-way communication. Internet enablement sales tools like Sales 2.0

provides you with 360 degrees wide range of visibility in an entire auto dealership and gives extensive ability to monitor functions such as service and maintenance, marketing, customer service as well as sales while still maintaining a customer-centric business module. It is also accessible from anywhere – on a train, in a restaurant or bus. This creates another golden-opportunity for return customers for renewal of insurance, replacement of vehicle parts and regularly checking on clients' pulsation.

Other Great Ways To Increase Your Visibility

7. **Placing your URL on all company materials** is a great way to gain the much needed visibility. Businesses capitalize on this free way to make their company known and transition it from good to a great one. All correspondences with suppliers and clients should bear the company details such as letterheads, promotional items, official company car and delivery vans. All emails being released into the stratosphere should equally bear the web domain, e-mail signature, signs and logos of the company so that this ensures the company's presence is felt by all those who they have dealings with it.

8. **Use of social media.** More traditional ways of selling are becoming less powerful; businesses are opting for social media to connect with customers and people who influence them to establish a brand name in the market place. It's a great way to exchange ideas with like-minded individuals, sharing of knowledge such as content of the company, culture and even news updates as well as word of mouth referrals. Radio and print are experiencing slow death as social media is taking the lead on virtually all sales and marketing channels. It's now about time to get acquainted with the use of **LinkedIn, Facebook** and **Twitter handles.** Scour LinkedIn and make contacts with people who make decisions like Senior Management, Deputy CEO's or even the CEO's or Chairmen of companies if they

happen to be known to you personally as they can also guide you along the corporate ladders on who can help you. It's also a forum to build a solid network by requesting to be introduced by your LinkedIn friends to people they seem to be already connected to. It pays off if you keep the messaging plain and simple. As you also build and gather points, have a good score on LinkedIn in-mail, and have enough followers on Twitter it turns out to be comparatively simple to connect or even better if people previously know of you or your name sounds pretty familiar for some good deeds in the recent past within the corporate corridors or even for some community service event.

For starters, LinkedIn in-mail is a good way to start off. The drawback could be that it could cost you in the initial stages and your limit on membership credits count could be low, nevertheless, if people you contact for some reason fail to respond within seven days, the credit is refunded to your membership account and can be utilized again.

Social media only works when it can be seen; therefore make it a point to focus on the niche clientele for your customers and prospects.

Good content and establishing a great presence are helpful in giving an impression for getting and keeping followers. It's important to include social media icons on your website such as; on the contact us page, homepage, blog, website footer etc. Be keen to add value to feeds from your followers in order to keep them. You have to continue adding value to your followers' feeds in order to retain them. Inclusion of official signature on e-mail and social media profiles keeps awareness alive to your online presence.

9. **You can also create a website for yourself** and put the address on your e-mail signature, poster presentations etc. so that people know where they can go to find out more about your work.
10. **Community Development Sponsorship.** Sponsoring a community project calls for availing of funds as well as willing members to participate in value added services to the chosen community. Every year, Barclays Bank PLC employees

reach out to the communities around the globe for voluntary involvement with the less privileged youth to help improve their entrepreneurial skills, increase their chances of working for a living, impart skills to enable them successfully run businesses and generally to help them get closer to their dreams. Barclays Bank PLC is committed towards social and financial issues and through an employee initiative called Make a Difference Day (MADD). MADD is a Barclays' Bank PLC annual volunteering campaign. I participated in 2009 MADD in a project in Likoni, Mombasa County, Kenya while at Barclays Bank PLC, Digo Road, Mombasa, Kenya where the then Managing Director & CEO, Aidan Mohamed then became the Cabinet Secretary (CS) for industrialization who was also in attendance. The event also enjoys media coverage in both local newspapers and National TV. It creates a positive impact involving all kinds of people from the community about the institution and is a great way to boost an organizations visibility.

11. **Be the Meeting Geek.** Devote three-minutes to seeking to know more of the next person's background. It's important that in all formal discussions, conference meetings, forums; they be concise, strictly keep time, be attentive, be definite, be well mannered and always request to know the next course of action. LinkedIn is powerful, get it to work for you, get intuition, and establish touch points, it's always important to give a keen ear than to rush for the sale. Look to provide a solution through comprehending the problems of the person you meet and engage in a discussion. Involve and get commitment from them and especially understand their thought pattern when trying to arrive at a possible solution, if that's what they are looking for, this becomes an easy sale, closing a sale long and hard is a thing of the past, as all the possibility of a mutually beneficial relationship can be lost forever.

12. **Request for an Introduction.** Every time you ask someone for an introduction always think about how you have related to them in the past. Principally consider the length you have

known them for, the last conversation you had, how close you have been to them over the years and incidences when they last made an introduction for you if any.

Be closely attentive to the following:

- Make is short and concise.
- Request a particular person.
- Be open, kind and non-hostile but precise.
- Topic of discussion is dependent on how closely you connect or associate.

Chapter 4

THE POWER OF CREDIBILITY; GETTING PEOPLE TO TRUST YOU

Getting people to trust your advice is a very important key element if you are looking to make a successful sales career. Countless seminars have given many myths on sales. First came the basics of establishing credibility – looking polished and professional, maintaining eye contact, being prepared every time, then it moved to closing skills which cost colossal amounts of money for companies to hire specialized consultants to impart these skills. The end result was that they were teaching salespeople to be smart salespeople and not trusted salespeople.

Most customers are duped into looking into other attributes of salespeople like a top of the range car and looking sharp in your dressing. Truth be said, nothing is as important as the depth of your credibility and this can be depicted from your polite mannerisms, integrity, product knowledge and just being trustworthy. Nothing is comparable to these virtues and if you are looking to maintain a great successful career, look no further!

The reality in today's market place is such that you have to come out as credible and a trusted advisor who solves customer's problems than to push product and services to prospects and customers. When you have positioned yourself as trustworthy and knowledgeable the customers buy YOU first before the product or even service.

The reason why most successful salespeople do well even when they change jobs from industry to industry is because they are trusted and people buy them first and not even the product or the company they represent.

According to Gerry Roberts in his book *"Millionaires mindset"*, the greatest persuasion for customers to purchase emanates from, in descending order of significance;

1. YOU
2. Product/Service
3. Company

Most companies include in their advertisements an overarching brand, elaborate logos, colors and core messages, but don't understand the main message that consumers have changed and your marketing strategy has not. They really do not care about you or the advertisements. If a company is interested in meeting the needs of the customers, fans and followers, then they should do it truly in a way that speaks to them. It therefore helps to understand how your customers think and feel about the company.

Companies develop their elaborate business plans, establish and introduce existence of their branding, companies opting for less traditional linkages such as social media platforms however, realize a few months down the line no one is buying from them! No one is opting to their email lists and wonder what could have happened? Customers don't trust us? Don't they think that we could bring value to them? How come there is less involvement with our brand, make or label? The answer is; all your color coding is attractive and superfluous, you have non-essential decorative features in promotional events, however, you are not credible enough.

How do you want your customers and clients to feel towards your company?

Lynda Shaw of Forbes magazine conducted a research by interviewing 25 CEO to get possible responses to the above question.

The responses were quite thought-provoking.

One of the CEO's wished his customers would view his business as genuine and honest-to-goodness with good moral standing. The most powerful burning desire the two others had was to make their customers have a low-risk perception of their business ingrained in them. Two others preferred their customers to inhibit risk-free feelings that their orders will be delivered in due time. Twenty of the remaining CEO's unanimously agreed the most important intuition from their customers would be that of *loyalty* to their brand.

This calls for a bit of hard work. To merit loyalty from customers you have secure their **trust**. Existing and prospective clients are always watchful and wide-awake waiting for salespeople to fall short of expectations. They are watching for improperly aligned information to the core values and mission statement of your company. They are faultfinding on the offers and bargains given and suspicious of a catch to it. They are constantly in search mode for a hint of misgiving and lack of certainty that they can cling onto that they can discerningly use as justification not to buy.

The contraposition of this is that when we triumph in securing their loyalty they will utterly and all-out defend their purchase decision for your products and services as they will not want it to be questioned. They become advocates for your products and services, loyal campaigner and the most trusted sales division.

It takes time and concerted efforts to build trust. However, here are some of the tips to establish trust, influence and credibility.

1. **Being Honest** should be common sense and take center stage. Should there be challenges, it's always good to address them promptly and with all honesty as this has become the common denominator of any flourishing business. These could include issue on service or product, tweet on your Twitter handle, post on Facebook etc. Needless to say, never overlook the community's influence on relationships. They are more resilient especially when they have been brought together under common terms such as trust, influence and credibility.

2. **Be Consistent in both Life and Business.** It's not possible to be that great hardworking and sociable individual at work and differ significantly in the community as an anti-social person who is also known to be a trouble maker. You are the same individual and should not inhibit such inconsistencies. Your offline behavior reflects your online success; therefore, it is important to be who you are as you are only one person at the end of the day. There is only one you, so be that person. It is therefore very important that the person you portray is objective, straightforward, truthful, impartial, unbiased, and sincere and one who interfaces closely with people on the job and off the job.

   "What you do off the job plays a major role in how far you go on the job. How many good books do you read each year? How often do you attend workshops? Who do you spend most of your time with?"

3. **Walk the Walk.** When you decide you are going to talk the talk, it's imperative for you to walk the walk. In other words, you have to act in a way that agrees with what you say. When you have made a proclamation that you are the leading social media and promotional marketing guru who is result oriented, your webpage, blog site as well as online persona should not look like a high school dropout developed it. Fix the fonts, fix the colors, and make it match with the content.

   Take the time to do what you say you are so good at doing. It's like a dietician who is 50 kilograms' overweight telling you that they don't worry about being healthy themselves, that they focus only on you. It's *absurd*. Any good agency, sales representative, consultant, business services provider should be doing for themselves what they say they can do for you.

If you don't take time to work on your own identity, sales processes, online persona, brand, website, content, business processes, why should anyone else believe you can do it for them? You are your own best proof and will be amazed at the number of clients you will attract if you start doing this today.

4. **It's of Paramount Importance to also Establish Authority.** You must know your stuff and demonstrate in depth understanding and knowledge of the subject matter. Faking it will not get you too far as customers will discover this sooner or later and you will not have a place in the market to hide your head. In the social realm it's easy to validate who you are, where you have worked, what references you have, who your clients are, who your contacts are and this can happen within a short time. It is far different than handing someone a business card. Your content on all social platforms must scream results. It must be obvious you know your stuff and prove you can deliver results. Give credit to your sources and never take other people's work as your own. Back up your claims with proof such as references, client testimonials, and more.

5. **Social Proof matters a Great deal.** No matter how much money you spend on details on a beautiful Twitter background, custom Facebook page and blog site, you still need to prove to be who and what you are. Take time to update online content at least once a month. Good examples of social proof include testimonials, partner references, customer references, links to work completed, kudos from other thought leaders, examples of work completed, guest blogs you have contributed to, links to blogs where you and your content has been cited, eBooks, etc. Social proof should be instantly available within one or less clicks on your site. One shouldn't have to dig, double and triple click to find it. Make it pop out from the front page. It's important just not to have what it takes, but also have a track record of performance that speaks for itself.

6. **Hang out with the Right Friends and Company.** Chances of being the 10th con when you spend most of your valuable time with 9 cons are very probable. Hang out with people you learn from, who build you, empower you and make you a better person. I attended one of Anthony Robbins' motivational workshops in Teecom, Media City, Dubai, U.A.E. on the 4th March, 2016 and he had this to say, "Whoever you spend time with, you become who they are." Avoid the people who kick you down, look down upon you, criticize you and overall envy your success. Be sure you hang around with the people who are going places. Establish real relationships and work together. Take time to know and research the people you hang out with. Don't just trust everyone on the first meeting. Just as you need to establish trust with your community, expect the same of those you bring into your inner circle.
7. **Take time and Invest in Relationships**. The deliberate act of commitment ends up differentiating you from the masses. Reach out to folks and people you are comfortable with and look up to. Visit places and forums which are positive spheres of influence such as a church group, community development group, volunteer group and organized groups etc. Become a member of your local Rotary club, be an active church member, join the debate club, join an evening cooking class. Get to interact and know folks in your local community and you will be on your way to establishing your own community.
8. **Body Language: Scientific interpretation.** Body language is important when it comes to making first impressions, forming new relationships and maintaining existing ones, which are some of the three things we do every day. Words account for 7% of the message, tone of voice takes 38% while body language accounts for 55%. Mastery of your tone of voice and body language combined takes the lion share at 93% of your message it's therefore an essential first step to building relationships and laying a great foundation based on trust.

Amy Cuddy, social psychologist and celebrated TED talker, (*TED {Technology, Entertainment, and Design} is a non-profit media organization which posts talks online for free distribution*) summed it up well as hereunder:

"Trust is the conduit for influence; it's the medium through which ideas travel. If they don't trust you, your ideas are just dead in the water. If they trust you, they're open and they can hear what you're offering. Having the best idea is worth nothing if people don't trust you."

9. **Writing a Book: Increases Your Visibility** A book bears sufficient proof and testament of your credibility in the market place and you can begin reaping the benefits of a book as a marketing tool.

   "Bottom line, When you're not trustworthy, your credibility, influence and business are lost as well." - Laban T. M'mbololo Esq.

   Writing a book not only enhances credibility but can also help to open doors which were previously closed or difficult to access. Salespeople who have authored books have used this to their advantage and use the book as a calling card and leave it with a customer or serious prospect. It helps a great deal in getting appointments and speaking engagements, builds rapport with clients and wins business.

   One major route to create credibility is through publishing a book. When you publicize a book, no matter if it's read or not it establishes instant respect and honor and people view you as an expert on the subject.

   In business people cling towards dealings with experts. Therefore, a publication is considered a great gimmick in establishing business connections and networks in the relevant industry. We more often than not seek solutions to problems, consult for expertise and proficiency and we also tend to associate with their accomplishments.

Writing a book broadens your reach. It spreads awareness of you and your business virally as people talk to each other about your book. Additionally, as you begin marketing and promoting your book, you will subsequently also be marketing and promoting your business. Your book and relevant marketing messages help your exposures to quickly add up. This means you will have more prospects who think highly of you when they have a need. And of course we are not only talking about how your book can help market your business. You can also use your book as a product or a bonus product to generate more sales. Whether you are selling it for a profit, giving it away to build a list, or using it as a strategic marketing tool, the better your book the more effective and successful it will be, so begin to visualize a great book with a well done artwork and graphics and it will surely do wonders.

There is no price tag you can put on trust. It is simply invaluable. Take the time to not only be a person people want to trust but ensure your persona helps you establish such.

10. **Connect with professionals online** - For most professionals, LinkedIn will be the most preferred platform. Salespeople meet a lot of individuals in their industry as well as other industries. By connecting with their prospects, after seeing them, salespeople are essentially demonstrating that they are well linked and networked. In this way, they are more likely to be perceived as an industry insider and this establishes their credibility and therefore not seen as a mere seller pushing goods or services.

Chapter 5

THE POWER OF AUTHORITY; GETTING YOUR PROPOSAL ACCEPTED AND BEING A POWER SELLER

Envisage a situation in your business where you could have your prospects buy faster! Imagine of a situation where you literally spend less time closing a sale and even cut the time by half and still be able to double your sales. It would be even better if you could get someone to sign up your prospects before you even meet them up.

It is important to stand out from the competition and position your brand as an authority in your industry, but how can you accomplish this effectively?

A good brand apart from providing direction and motivation enhances the net worth of a company and makes customer acquisition effortless as its considered special and what customers hold in high esteem. Brands over a span of period create trust because they meet the customer's expectations and therefore reputed for their attributes of specifications and consistency.

A good brand will possess the following four features:

1. Uniqueness. (Red Cross logo is universal, it's ingrained into our collective consciousness and we associate it with medical assistance.)
2. Consistency. (Coca cola is displayed using the same iconic logo which is cursive, elicits similar emotions of positivity, authenticity and inclusiveness)
3. Relevance. (Uber taxis don't use as much gas as SUV's and other fuel guzzlers, and are therefore economical and dependable rides.)
4. Connects customers with an emotion (iPhone, the brand value permeates through absolutely everything, from usability to design.)

A brand is considered superior. When individuals, ideologies, abstract forms, exhibit the features of a brand it's relatively simple and trouble-free to sell it to the would-be end users. The same concept applies to people. Such an individual can be relied upon and is seen as one who is always prepared, is a team player, has a positive attitude and is an achiever; everyone knows what to anticipate. An individual, who has created a brand, can be trusted to work well with others and achieve great results.

A sudden variation or difference could spell adversities. Take the instance of Mercedes-Benz whose origins date back to 1926 when the first car bearing its signature brand appeared. Mercedes-Benz have established themselves as a reputable and trusted brand for years and are known for style which is very sophisticated, coupled with exhilarating performance and ingenious technology. If thousands of Mercedes-Benz cars suddenly began malfunctioning, clients would opt not to purchase the Mercedes-Benz. If they learnt of a sudden adverse change in these circumstances it could as well mean damage to their reputation built over all the years and what the customers have held dear to their hearts for ages.

Valuable Lessons from High performing Sales Rep

Visualize going out to meet a client or prospect without bringing in product samples and not using all the sales paraphernalia. Do not go as a marketer – go in as a friend, offering a probable solution after listening to the client, understanding their problem and thinking pattern. Leaving out your tools of trade for once will make an impact and establish utmost trust. Most salespeople are too eager to show off their knowledge and start talking about the features, advantages and benefits (FAB approach) of the product before listening to the customer and in this way, they seem like a doctor giving prescription before actually interviewing a patient and getting a proper diagnosis.

> *"Motivation fuels the attitude that builds the confidence necessary to sustain the persistence."*

1. **Customers put their interests first, not yours** Most companies run advertisements that include the company name, company logo, brand core message and headline, that are of no interest to the customers they seek to influence. Customers have changed but the marketing strategy has not changed, they do not care about you and do not take notice of your advertisements.

    According to author Kelley Robertson some of the following real life situations will guarantee results if adopted correctly by salespeople.

    "Mark Bozzini, CEO of Infinite Spirits, learned a powerful selling lesson early in his career. His job was to sell more bottles of wine than were sold the previous year, which was not a daunting task. However, when he called on a wine and spirits retailer, the storeowner told him that his products were not selling and he would rather not have them on his shelves. A typical salesperson would become pushy, or even leave and decide to seek a sale elsewhere. But Bozzini, an intuitive and passionate salesman, was determined to make the sale. He spent an hour rearranging the display of the store and asked the storeowner to give it a chance to see if the product sold better. The new display worked the trick, and the storeowner became one of Bozzini's best customers." Inspiration we get from this narrative is that: *"the customer doesn't care about your interests. They care more about their own interests"*

> *"Success is knowing the difference between cornering people and getting them in your corner" – Bill Copeland*

2. **It's All About Value Creation**

"Salespeople are value creators." If you visit a Safaricom retail outlet (a subsidiary of Vodafone UK) practically most of the time they are overwhelmed with clients. They are professionals with expert knowledge on different products ranging from computers, phones, software's from different manufacturers as well as accessories. These experts want to establish the salient features of what you need telephony or computing that fits your requirements and is passionate to you. To build confidence as well as trust with their customers, different departments have been established to attend to specific issues to assure Safaricom customers will at all times reach someone helpful with solutions to their queries or problems. Even when Safaricom decides to charge a premium rate for its products and services, they are still assured it will create a rush and therefore demand and more often than not with long customers' queues lining up till close of business for that day. It's no wonder they are making super profits.

> *"Check the records. There has never been an undisciplined person who was a champion. Regardless of the field of endeavor, you'll find this to be true." – Zig Ziglar*

3. **The Power of an Emotional Connection**

   This is just a recap of what was earlier reiterated at the beginning of Chapter 5. These are the salient features of a brand which are powerful in creating an emotional connection with an esteemed clientele; Uniqueness (Red Cross logo is universal, it's ingrained into our collective consciousness and we associate it with medical assistance). Consistency (Coca cola is displayed using the same iconic logo which is cursive, elicits similar emotions of positivity, authenticity and inclusiveness). Relevance (Uber taxis don't use as much gas as SUV's and other fuel guzzler's, and are therefore economical and dependable rides). The creation of such an emotional connection is what creates brand ambassadors, gets reviews done online, business gets transacted by word of mouth referrals, fans become excellent advocates and assume the salespeople's responsibilities

   "When you choose to be pleasant and positive in the way you treat others, you have chosen, in most cases, how you are going to be treated by others"

4. **The Power of Selling from Successful Brands**

   Emotion Sells

   In the new world, successful selling is not what you do with a customer, it is something you do with the customer since the customer has a voice and is involved in the whole sales process.

   Brand + Selling = Success

   But just what role does a brand play in a selling strategy? It's not usually noticeable but a chosen brand becomes an extremely powerful selling tool and significantly influences the decision to purchase the item such as a drink etc.

Did you ever consider why the salespeople at Starbucks are called baristas instead of employees? Howard Schultz, the chief executive officer of Starbucks, has built the brand in his vision since the company began in 1982. He believes strongly that the brand stands for more than beans. During an interview, he said, "By making a deeper emotional connection with your customers, your brand will stand out from the hundreds, if not thousands, of vendors, entrepreneurs, and business owners selling similar services and products." Schultz is especially passionate about the role salespeople have in creating the "Starbucks" experience. The brand recently launched a new marketing promotion termed as, "It's not just coffee. It's Starbucks." When you hear what these brand ambassadors talk about it emanates from an emotional connection to the Starbucks brand.

> *"You get the best out of others when you give the best of yourself – Harvey Firestone"*

Why Starbucks rather than another café? Starbucks is by far powerful and its brand presence therefore is more predominant than any competitor.

5. **Willingness to Take Risks: Good for Business**

Does this sound familiar? "You won't know until you try". This affirmation is actually factual with reference to sales. The willingness to take risks makes the distinction. Reflect on the risk levels you indulge in your daily life and the results thereof. A practical illustration is when salespeople decide to cold call CEO's and top brass corporate management members previously unknown to them, networking and meeting individuals of high net worth (HNW) is littered with considerable risks. The roadmap to attaining success is found by getting out of your comfort zone (safety net or buffer zone). I can personally attest to this. In 2015 when I was still very green in Dubai, I came across a business opportunity in high-end hotel apartments. As much as it was not in my area of expertise I decided to give it a try. All I got was discouragement from friends. They retorted that it was no mean feat and that offshore real estate was indeed not for the fainthearted. Despite the circumstances I believed in myself and knew success wasn't too far away. I went on to become the first person to introduce the Dubai based offshore property company to the Kenyan market and on the 11th January, 2018 on my birthday I was pleasantly surprised with a call from the Senior Business Development, West Africa informing me of my first sale of an offshore property from one of my clients in Kenya. This called for celebration and was a real reason to roister.

Lisa McCullough, a lady professional in stunts summarized it by saying: "Focus not on your worries, concentrate on your goals"

> "The biggest risk is not taking any risk… In a world that's changing really quickly, the only strategy that is guaranteed to fail is not taking risks. –Mark Zuckerberg"

6. The Power of Persistence

As Robert Half coined it, "Persistence is what makes the impossible possible, the possible likely, and the likely definite." How does this apply in the marketplace? Most salespeople give up too early. For one to actually stop pursuing a prospect they need to have followed them up between 7-9 times. It's important to strike a balance and follow up with a call to the prospect at least once a week and on each occasion giving more additional information about the product or service e.g. discount offer or a reduction in price that could persuade the prospect to buy your product or service.

What I can attest from my own experience is from a client I followed up for nearly seven months. I had made good first impressions and I was sure I would land the deal. Clients can be difficult and can pose some questions that require more than just knowledge, this calls for a finer oil grade; **experience**. You need to be wary of this and well prepared in case such questions pop up and one wrong answer could send the deal spiraling and make it slip out of your hands. I tenaciously visited the client and each time rendered more useful information than on my previous visit. In November, 2018 the patience paid off and lady luck was also on my side as I was able to seal the deal which was a massive order for cross-border sourcing for building and construction materials for 36 apartments from the People's Republic of China (P.R.C.) to Kenya.

"Nothing in this world can take the place of persistence. Talent will not…. Determination and persistence alone are omnipotent." - John Calvidge Coolidge Jnr

7. **The Power of Adapting Your Approach**

Concentrate on directing your clients towards attaining outcomes and objectives. Grant them control over sales discussions and during presentations, request for their points of view, and allow them to share their ideologies and thinking patterns. You will easily gain their acceptance. Avoid a lot of chit-chat in your discussions, these are busy people and would want to get down to business and close deals swiftly. Don't shy away even when they get brutal and straightforward with you, and most importantly retain high confidence levels throughout the sales process.

"The ability to connect with people is a key sales trait."- Kelley Robertson

8. **The Power of Affirmations**

Being confident is a key element to success in sales, but it's not always easy to feel this way. Developing the skill of using positive self-talk or affirmations can boost not only your self-image, but also your success in your job. An affirmation is a powerful tool that will help you in developing personal self-confidence, reprogram your thinking, and achieve better results. Simply put, affirmations are positive statements that we repeat to ourselves frequently. Although many people are familiar with this concept, few actually use it on a regular basis. In one of Anthony Robbins workshop that I attended in Teecom, Media City, Dubai, UAE, he famously proclaimed that incantations said to yourself repeatedly could change your habits and break through your worry habits. To change anything in your life it only takes 10% of the conscious mind to convince 90% of your subconscious mind to do anything you have ever imagined possible.

How does this apply in sales? If your goal is to attain US$10,000 in sales, this has to be broken into smaller realizable amounts in an incremental manner. If you just set it to say US$8,000 the conscious mind will not accept it and will have a problem processing this as a reality. Instead start with achieving US$3,500 then create an affirmation of US$6,500 once the earlier set goal has been achieved.

You can use affirmations to develop self-confidence in selling. Repeat these statements aloud to yourself several times a day and you will soon notice a change in your behavior. Before we can succeed in achieving the set goal we must magnetize our minds with intense desire for achieving the goal and become goal conscious until the desire creates definite plans for achieving this goal of US$10,000 in sales.

> *"It's the repetition of affirmations that leads to belief. And once that belief becomes a deep conviction, things begin to happen."*
>
> *- The Believing Magic*

9. **The Power of a Personal Appearance**

   Whether we like it or not, our appearance will affect our sales results. That does not mean you have to dress in a two-thousand-dollars suit, but it is critical that you look professional regardless of what you sell. My personal belief is that you should dress one step higher than your client. It is easier to tone down your appearance during a meeting by removing your jacket or tie than it is to step it up.

   "We tend to evaluate others on the basis of physical, outward appearance."

   -Marvin J. Ashton

10. **The Power of Asking for Help**

    No one can achieve true success or full potential on his or her own. We all need other people to help us along the way. However, the majority of salespeople do not ask for assistance, and try to do everything themselves. A client once said this, "Prior to starting my business, I contacted many other people who operated similar businesses. I wanted to know what challenges they encountered, what mistakes they made, and what advice they would give someone who was beginning a business. Everyone I contacted was helpful and willing to share his or her experiences. I took notes and referred to them as I planned my strategy. I also read dozens of books that were related to my business. Last, I approached a well-respected businessperson, discussed my plans with him, and asked his advice. I listened carefully to what he told me and worked at implementing his ideas. Several years later, I constantly talk to other sales professionals, small business owners, sales trainers and authors. I have learned that I don't know everything. (Ouch! That was hard to admit!) However, I do know that I want to be successful in my business, and talking to other people gives me additional insights."

"If you don't swallow your pride and you try to tough it out in an area where you lack skill, knowledge or experience, you exponentially increase the likelihood you will fail."
                                        -Dave Lorenzo, Career Intensity

11. The Power of Articles

Writing articles is one of the most effective ways to establish yourself as an expert. Articles give you great exposure both in print and online, and writing an article is more than you think. Most trade publications are hungry for content. Kelley Robertson once said this. "When my first book was released, I was contacted by a trade magazine to write a regular column for them. Since then, I have expanded my writing and now submit articles to several hundred publications—paper and web-based. I have booked many workshops and speaking engagements as a direct result of someone reading one of these articles. You may feel that this strategy does not apply to your industry. I know many people who write, including real estate agents, people who sell vending services, financial planners, marketing experts, professional speakers, virtual assistants, publicists, retailers, health-supplement manufacturers, just to name a few. Regardless of what you sell and to whom, articles can help you get noticed by prospective customers. Writing articles can help you establish yourself as an expert. However, any article you write must address the concerns of your target market. This means that you need to consider what problems your target audience faces and write an article that offers suggestions to deal with these issues". You may also feel that you can't write a lengthy article that people will read. Here are some tips that will help you get started:

a) Start with a main point or topic. Let's say you sell industrial farm equipment. You could easily write articles about proper maintenance of the equipment, as well as some tips and techniques to maximize the use and life span of specific products. Your article could be, *Eight Ways to Extend the Life of Your Tractor.*

b) Think of six or eight key points that are relevant to your topic. The average article in a trade magazine is six hundred to one thousand words, so write a hundred words (about two paragraphs) for each key point. Using the tractor example, you would elaborate on each of the eight ways to extend the life of a tractor. In some cases, you will find that you can write an entire article about one single point.

c) Create an opening or introduction, and close with a call to action. Write in a conversational tone rather than a formal one. It can help if you picture the typical person who will be reading the article and imagine that you are writing to that person.

d) Write a byline or author bio that states who you are what you do and for whom, and how to contact you—telephone and e-mail. You're done! You will find that it is easier to write at certain times than others.

"My aim is to put down on paper what I see and what I feel in the best and simplest way."
-Ernest Hemingway

12. The Power of Elevator Speeches

"The real art of conversation is not only to say the right thing at the right place but to leave unsaid the wrong thing at the tempting moment." – Dorothy Neville

Formulate a Killer "Elevator Speech" Which Screams Sales Results

The quickest method to get clients and advocates for your business is to hit the ground running and embark on networking and referral marketing. For this to work effectively you will have to know how to respond when the conversation boils down to, "… what's YOUR profession or what do YOU do for a living?"

Communicating in short, impactful sound bites is an essential part of everyday life, and effectively speaking about our talents and capabilities — also known as the "elevator speech" — is an important part of making a great first impression. You must be self-aware and introspective and have a clear sense of the image you wish to portray. For example, are you looking to network, are you trying to find the next piece of business or seeking a new job? You simply cannot adopt a kitchen-sink approach.

> *"There are always three speeches, for every one you actually gave. The one you practiced, the one you gave, and the one you wish you gave." – Dale Carnegie*

When done right, elevator speeches can provide a simple, memorable and impactful way to make a first impression. We must strive to look for ways to leverage the coincidence that present themselves in our lives to create more opportunities to meet and get to know people better, both on and off the elevator.

13. Use Power of the 73% Factor to Your Favor to Get Appointments

> *"Don't make such decisions whose bad results make you look like you are your own enemy." - Amit Kalantri*

Approximately about 73% of all people according to author Kelley Robertson can't make instant decisions. Start making phone calls to prospects and utilize the 73% aspect to work in your favor in booking business. Provide 2 different timings or schedules for your meet ups. It gives relief to the other party and puts you in a position of power and authority over the discussion, and what remains is firming up on a time to meet up.

In order for this approach to materialize, it should take less than 20 seconds. During this time it's important to respond to the questions anybody picking their phone would intuitively query. Who's on the other line? What's the purpose of their phone call? The following is an illustration on the 20 seconds phone call. Good Morning Mr. John, I'm David of Lloyds Bank Plc. (Answers Q1.) I wish to share an amazing opportunity to be a lucky winner of a free business tour to Guangzhou, China for the people holding active business accounts for at least last 5 years running. (Answers Q2.) Would tomorrow afternoon 11:15pm be good or would 3:30pm be more appropriate?

14. **The Power of the Telephone Factor**

"This was before voice mail, recorded phone messages you can't escape. Life was easier then. You just didn't pick up the phone." - Joyce Carol Oates, Beasts

Attack Fear of Calling Prospects Head-On. Salespeople have imminent fears of calling prospects for business. Confessions of timidity and acting on them are a good beginning. The act of getting on the telephone unleashes enormous energy. The moment you start getting affirmative responses, it gives you an inner conviction to go on and you discover you are actually in control of your future. When your appointments start to show affirmative responses and you begin to book business, you begin to feel better and the fact that you have actually combated your fears and put them behind you.

There is an imminent fear that engulfs salespeople that makes them make fewer phone calls than they should when chasing for business. Professional sales trainers put a lot of emphasis on the relation between the prospect and salespeople but often do not talk about the "the third man". The question is, who is *"the third man"*? The third man actually represents *"The trouble thoughts."*

These are fear feelings which are common and manifest in all salespeople who have to get past these feelings. It dissuades you from making the call at that very instant when you are required to and gives you an inner conviction to wait and make the sales call at a supposedly better time.

Use Answering machine Messages to "Read" Prospects. When playing messages from the answering machine or voicemail, this presents an excellent opportunity to figure out the caller. Is he humorous? Is she a fast or slow-paced speaker? The talking pace can depict many things about their character and how to even speak to them in a similar tone when returning their calls and "mirror" their characters.

Voicemail greetings can be an incredible conversation technique for your business phone. Set up the right voicemail greetings to impress your customers and prospects. Your caller must have a very good reason to reach out to you, therefore every reason to make them feel welcome and attended to.

Call Decision-Makers, Professionals and Executives before or after Business hours or during lunch.

Decision makers often start earlier and work later than employees. The odds of reaching these people rise dramatically if you call them early in the morning, late in the day, or during lunch. Secretaries and assistants are not usually around to screen calls at these times of the day, so the decision maker will answer his or her phone calls. In addition, Executives will not have their voice mail system activated during these times.

15. **How to Use the Power of Silence**

Silence if used appropriately in sales can sanction more power than words could ever say. Salespeople don't use this technique very often. Silence unsettles people and others prefer not to implore it to work for them.

"Nothing strengthens authority so much as silence" – *Leonardo da Vinci, artist and innovator*

Most salespeople are guilty of talking too much thinking they will be considered brilliant and would be able to close a sale much faster. The truth is such that the sooner you exercise silence, the quicker you will start to get affirmative responses. When you pose a question to a prospective client don't be afraid to stop at the question mark. Ask the question and stop. Refrain from giving more explanations after the question; it may end up diluting not only the question but also the power of the message.

When to use silence to make business decisions?

1. **How to Handle Client Objections and Queries.** The often made mistake is responding too soon to questions. There is no law forbidding the use of silence. How do you respond to objections raised by a client? For example if a client retorts, "your items are very highly priced." All you require is a moment of silence and the client will need to fill in the silence with the reasons why they feel you are too pricy and they will end up volunteering the information you needed to give an informed response. No matter how uncomfortable you may feel with some seconds of silence, but just hold it right there. If you are on a conference meeting, don't respond to all the questions raised, response to one or two questions will suffice. If you use too many words, the point of view you intend to make can get lost. Exercising silence at this point gives you the opportunity to be heard when it matters the most.
2. **The Biggest Secret of Negotiation.** Silence used in the negotiation process can be nerve-racking. When the buyer is silent, it makes you wonder about their thought patterns.

Turn-the-table and be silent and let them wonder what it is that you are thinking about. For example, if the buyer mentions the price they want to pay, don't respond at once. Don't say, "That's fine" or "No", go for an extended pause instead. The silence will cause discomfort to the buyer and they will want to fill in the void and begin speaking, hence revealing information that will give you a domineering position to move the conversation forward.

3. **Silence When Closing a Business Deal** Sometimes talking too much becomes our downfall, and wanting to be seen as smart ends up making us do silly and costly mistakes. When sitting down with a prospect, more often than not, we are better off when we talk less. The technique is more of getting the client *interested* rather than being *interesting*. Once we have included all the details, facts and figures in the proposed client solution, we should embark on silence by allowing several seconds to elapse and let the prospect be the next one to talk. This is referred to as *the silent close*. It not only exudes your confidence by not talking to prove your point, but also provides the prospect with a window of opportunity to exercise their purchasing resolution.

"The right word may be effective, but no word was ever as effective as a rightly-timed pause – Mark Twain"

16. The Unbelievable Power of Storytelling

"A story is a way to say something that can't be said in any other way." – Flannery O'Connor

Storytelling is what brings us together, defines us and at the same time sets us apart. Storytelling allows us to make a connection with each other, get genuinely known and gain recognition. Stories today have become an integral part of business sales presentation or PowerPoint PPT talk which is a solid business tool necessary for addressing a gathering.

Storytelling emotionalizes information and exceeds mere transmission of data and facts. More often than not, there are 69% chances that a gathering will recall a storytelling incidence more than anything else said since they bring emotive feelings and a connection with the mind. Storytelling seizes the moment and is not comparable to the monotonous and tedious PowerPoint PPT talks that have become part and parcel of business.

The way to make a long-term impression and make it linger in the mind is through storytelling. Below herein please find 5 reasons why storytelling is solid business dissemination artillery:

a) Stories are our preferred mode of accepting news, knowledge, facts and figures. Stories permeate our lives and give a connection and make us recall things easily.
b) Storytelling establishes a solid, positive response and has bodily influence on us. Our endocrine system secretes "feel-good chemicals" during the storytelling session when we expect a happy ending to the story.
c) Stories go where mere data and analytics can't go. Stories assist the hearer in pointing out personalities and establishing a personal relationship.
d) Stories change how we view people. It also helps others realize our importance and comprehend that we mean well.
e) Stories persuade. It results in an in-depth relationship and also demonstrates our view-points and gets us straight to the point.

Stories are especially powerful in sales as we try to cut through the noise of an information-overloaded world. Here are some ideas for bringing the power of stories into your selling approach:

- Disseminate a factual narrative that establishes your view-point and fortifies your intentions.
- Intertwine potential of an organization's great history into your sales pitch.

- Utilize storytelling to relate with the prospects and demonstrate how the product offerings meet their requirements, and offer value-added solutions.

17. The Power of Time Management

"The secret of getting ahead is getting started. The secret of getting started is breaking your complex overwhelming tasks into manageable tasks, and then starting on the first one." – Mark Twain

Have you ever wished for a few more hours in a day? Why is it that some people seem to get everything done effortlessly and others feel that time constantly eludes them?

According to Elle Harrington a wellness, corporate and private coach the secret to managing your time well isn't working more hours. It is about prioritizing the important things and learning to use the time you have more efficiently and effectively. The secret is working smarter, not harder.

Some of us, by nature, organize and get tasks out of the way before we relax, while others of us play first and work later. It is important to first recognize which type you are and whether your style is allowing you to have the life you really want.

Maybe you are super-organized at work, but burn out because you don't know how to make time for yourself. Maybe you are naturally a less organized person who knows how to relax, but you are dissatisfied because you aren't fulfilling your goals and dreams.

Rather than labeling yourself or beating yourself up, realize that time management is an area of your life that you can strengthen. Like a new muscle, it takes practice and repetition to make it stronger.

Point to note to streamline your day;

- Assign time schedules for organizing and planning.
- Rank tasks in order of urgency and begin with the top-most on the list.
- By close-of-business, prepare a written "things-to-do" list for the preceding day, so it's out of your mind and also in adherence to the employer's clean-desk policy.
- Establish a reasonable "things-to-do" list that is not too daunting. Only follow a single list at a time.
- Get rid of non-essential duties.
- Add on one third (1/3rd) allowances onto the duration a task will normally take to cater for disturbances or unforeseen emergencies.
- Allocate the duration in a manner that minimizes disturbances and your rate of production.
- Perform vital tasks preferably during the day when you supposedly have the highest energy levels as per your biological prime time.
- Begin rejecting all duties dumped at your desk, don't be a YES MAN.
- Request for assistance and assign duties.
- Pat yourself on the back every day for tasks successfully completed.

These are the two greatest impediments in utilizing time proficiently: *postponement* and *purposelessness*. There's a tendency of postponement upon realization that the task at hand appears challenging, demoralizing or mean-looking and feel it's a tone of responsibility that is non-executable. This can cause the "deer in the headlights" experience and this is a clear indication that "chunking" would be an option. The is the deliberate act of either splitting the roles into more manageable tasks or delegating and assigning to more people for effective execution, but remember always to begin with the top-most on the list duties in terms of urgency.

"Am I doing what I love to do? Am I doing something meaningful to myself?" are some of the questions that ring at the back of your mind that cause the task to feel dull, monotonous and tedious when you are not managing your time effectively. Effective people insist on the importance to incorporate perception of the future to create a driving force for accomplishing the tasks you consider mundane and therefore routine.

Your focal-point should be organization, so duties are executed in an effective and efficient manner which leads to a more balanced, jubilant and exhilarating life that frees up time for exercises and relaxation which are important in rejuvenation of your mind and body as well as uplifting your spirits.

18. The Power of Thank You Cards

> *"Thanksgiving is possible only for those who take time to remember; no one can give thanks that have a short memory."* - Anonymous

Establishing linkages and networks is the order of the day in sales. Come up with an objective to mail ten "thank you notes" on a daily basis. Mail them to individuals you encounter, showcase product-offering to, call often and those you provide assistance to regularly. Turn into a "thank you note" nut or fanatic.

Are you ready for this? After three years of continuous selling, business will be flourishing and 98% of all deals booked will be entirely on client referrals. The persons you have been showing gratefulness and indebtedness will be glad to provide quality referrals as a token of appreciation for making them feel great and distinguished. Astonishing, right?

Below herein are examples of thank you notes to send to your prospects and customers as depicted by Tom Hopkins.

a) **Contact, Telephone Number.** Much appreciation for speaking to me. In this new world order time is invaluable. I ascertain to always remain considerate of your time resource as we deliberate on the probability of meeting your requirements.
b) **Contact, In-person** Much appreciation. I was delighted to connect with you. And my appreciation goes out for the time we spent together. We have been privileged to offer services to many satisfied customers and it's my hope to offer you valuable service in the near future.
c) **Post-Exhibition/ Display/ Show.** Much appreciation for the chance to deliberate on your requests in the near future. We will be esteemed to offer you our service now and always. We have no doubt that our standards, combined with distinguished assistance, is the basis of a fruitful relationship.
d) **Post-Purchase.** Much appreciation for the chance to provide our exquisite service assistance. We are certain that you will be pleased with our recent_____. My objective is to provide outstanding post sales service assistance so that you will have the conviction of offering me client referrals with identical requirements to yours.
e) **Received a Client Reference.** Much appreciation for client reference to Mark and Dorothy Mwakio. I can guarantee that all your client references will get the distinguished competent service assistance possible.
f) **Post-Resistance.** Much appreciation for allowing me to offer beneficial service to you. It's with heartfelt dismay that I'm presently not able to help you. Nevertheless, if you require additional details or have queries, kindly do not hesitate to contact me. I will be glad to share any upcoming developments and/or modifications that will be of help to you.
g) **Post-Purchase from Competitor.** Much appreciation for sparing time to consider our product-offering. I'm sorry I can't

show you the advantages we provide at this particular time. I will contact you and wish that we will be able to transact in the near future.

h) **Post-Purchase from Competitor, and provide Client References.** Much appreciation for polite consideration to provide client references. As earlier deliberated, I am attaching three of my visiting/business cards. I'm grateful for directing them in the palms of three of your close companions, associates and relations that I could provide service to. I will contact you and I'm ready to provide assistance as required.

i) **To Someone that Provides Assistance.** Much appreciation. I'm delighted to connect with a devoted person providing valuable service. Your endeavors are genuinely recognized. If our organization or I can render service in any way, kindly feel free to contact me.

j) **Commemoration Appreciation.** My appreciation. It is with best wishes that I extend my greetings and once more, express gratitude for your continued support. Kindly contact me if you have any queries concerning your_____ or the recent developments in the latest versions.

The potential power of a conveyed appreciation is substantial. Get this weapon to work wonders for you Now!

19. Why Product Knowledge is Power

"Today knowledge has power. It controls access to opportunity and advancement.
-Peter Drucker"

Product knowledge refers to better understanding of a product or service offering and the collection of pertinent information about its attributes, operational features as well as its applicable uses. Thorough product knowledge, leads to better dissemination of product information to prospects and clients on how it will address their needs and this transmutes into greater sales. Below herein are the advantages of superior product knowledge as depicted by Mathew Hudson;

a) **Strong Communication.** Good knowledge concerning a product gives authority to the retailer to exercise various techniques and vary them as appropriate to convey the brand message of the product to the different prospects and clients which can be a tremendous sales boost.
b) **Enthusiasm to Increase Productivity.** Demonstrating enthusiasm about a product offering is very comforting as it gives an edge over other salespeople. When you create elation for a product, you eliminate any misgivings on the product and services among the prospects and clients which provokes more sales.
c) **Boosts your Confidence.** When a client is not committal to closing a sale, this could emanate due to absence of confidence demonstrated by a sales person. Being well informed on the product attributes automatically exudes confidence and gets deals booked faster.
d) **The Secret to Overcoming Objections.** When customers raise objections the best way to counter them is by providing reveling and fact-based information. Having this superior knowledge base in not only your products but even those of the competitors could help sway sales in your favor.

Product Knowledge: More Sales

Here are some of the sources of product knowledge: Understanding sales and marketing literature, discussions with salespeople, thorough training, and role playing for success, managing objections, practical use and testimonials.

Vital information such as the production process, importance of the product as well as its uses, what it can blend and work well with.

Pertinent Details that you should Know on Products:

- Market pricing structure
- Colors, styles and available versions
- A brief history of the product lifecycle
- Manufacturing: materials and complex processes
- Uses of the product and services
- Channels of distribution, logistics and wholesaling
- Warranty or repair information

It may take a while to easily articulate your product knowledge, especially with new products, but over time you will become comfortable and confident in providing the correct information to shoppers. That confidence will pay off in improved sales results.

20. The Power of Punctuality

"Punctuality is not just limited to arriving at a place at the right time; it is also about taking actions at the right time." - Amit Kalantri

Punctuality is a whole mark of a disciplined sales officer, are you one? This entails being where you are intended to be, at a specified time, without excuses, as and when required. Sincerity and timeliness are latently intertwined.

Arriving where you are supposed to be punctually provides you with the liberty to assume and command others to behave with civility towards you. It's not possible to expect others to behave with civility towards you in regards to time when you disregard theirs; you don't possess grip, power and influence over that. The one who observes punctuality has a whip-hand and an edge over other personnel, suppliers as well as customers.

Chapter 6

YOU KNOW YOU ARE AT THE TOP WHEN.....

You Know How To Strike a Work-Life Balance

If you are in pursuit of an accomplished career and a joyous and invigorating family, you will need to strike a balance. This translates into prioritizing matters of greater importance first, reaching well thought out decisions ahead of time, and proficient use of time as a resource.

According to Queensland government striking a balance between work and life is attained by setting the right daily schedules to achieve equilibrium between toil and personal living. The gains than ensue from achieving this desired balance comprise of:

a) Improved job motivation and work attitudes.
b) Enhances concentration and focus.
c) Better health or well-being.
d) Less home and workplace stress intensities.
e) More involvement in parenting, community inclusion and ability to monitor development of children closely.
f) Ample time for relationships, hobbies and other personal projects.

How do you maintain good work-life balance?

A great way to do this is by envisioning what legacy you would want to leave behind and spill over these thoughts and have it manifested in your daily life. Frequent review and assessment of your priorities items is certainly the best way to balance the dictates of a tight-scheduled life.

Ways to encourage healthy work-life equilibrium:

a) Put down objectives in the order of their importance.
b) Proficient control of time – analyze work schedules, most pressing matters, and success factors.
c) Establish clear guidelines between work and personal life. Don't carry work home.
d) Establish flexibility and adopt an optimistic outlook.
e) Keep away from pressure and strain, emotional collapse, and exhaustion – weariness reduces your production levels.
f) Keep up healthful living – take care of yourself, consume nourishing foods, have enough rest and spend some time keeping fit or doing something fulfilling.
g) Obtain great mutual assistance – master the art of delegation, at times we require a helping hand.
h) Get a buzz out of your job.

"There is no work-life balance. We have one life. What's most important is that you be awake for it." - Janice Marturano

You Set and Review your SMART Goals

An attribute that distinguishes successful people from failures, is the simple fact; they have their life goals inscribed on paper. Most people can't be bothered. Ideally, these individuals wander in life pointlessly, puzzled about their life's purposelessness and even sometimes loose the passion of living it. Having your life- goals written is the beginning of great things, but certainly it's not the be-all end-all.

Revelations of the Harvard Yale famous study were such that; of the entire 1953 graduating class, only 3% had their goals in writing with a correlating plan for execution. A sequel and re-examination study that was conducted 20 years later in 1973, the disclosure was such that the 3% who in fact had their goals written were happier, well-heeled and affluent as well as more physically fit than their fellow classmates, and as a matter of fact had amassed 97% of the total wealth of that class.

According to Michael Hyatt a *New York Times* bestselling author, the magic upon which the most important things are completed successfully lies in having written goals. The significance is outlined in the 5 reasons as hereunder;

1. **Personal Vision Statement: What do You Want to Achieve?** This is equivalent to embarking on a journey without the destination in mind. What do you carry in your luggage? Which route will you use? How do you know you have arrived at your destination? Ideally, you begin with the *end* in mind. The same can be said of life achievements. Putting down your goals in a written form compels you to figure out the end results and exactly what is to be done in between.
2. **Motivate Yourself to Take Action.** After writing goals the next essential course of action lies in expressing them, though this doesn't end here. Success lies in taking action. Written goals and their subsequent review have the effect of captivating you to swing into action.
3. **Filter of Hope.** Prosperity attracts more openings and opportunities until such a time you become swamped and could even get derailed. The answer lies in reviewing your goals often to find out if they are within the plans.
4. **Overcoming Resistance to Your Success.** Even the most cherished desires, aspirations and objectives meet with opposition. This begins the moment a goal is set. The focus

should remain goal-achievement not the underlying obstacles, that's the only way to get past them.

5. **Things That Will Help You Celebrate Your Progress.** Life is not a bed of roses (Life is tribulation and cross). The hard part lies in when you don't seem to see any headway. There is this feeling of throwing good after bad; you can't get what you want. Writing goals has a way of punctuating your road-map to success with mile-posts (waymark), which are indicators of how much is done and what is left to the destination. Reaching the end is usually a cause for celebration!

Attaining exceptional success in life has something to do with having goals written on paper and the reason why this forms a very significant task that you should embark on without further ado if you haven't already done that.

> *"If you have built castles in the air, your work need not be lost; that is where they should be. Now put the foundations under them." - Henry David Thoreau*

You stay Physically Fit

Sales is a demanding profession, make it a point to integrate a healthy lifestyle coupled with a good fitness program. Below herein are some of the benefits you may derive.

- Feel better physically and mentally
- Gets you to focus on duties you are thrilled to perform
- Look better, feel even better
- Decrease your risk of disease
- Help avoid injuries

Affirmative results are a function of a good fitness and routine program, a feeling of importance and self-worth, better sleep patterns, less stress levels, as well as better relationships and social cohesion.

"Healthy citizens are the greatest asset any country can have."
- Winston S. Churchill

You Know The Time Value of Today

You will acknowledge the fact that today will never come back again, and therefore it's vital that we value our time; arise early, and start well and accomplish what we set out to do every day.

   i. **Personal Life Values.** Making a conscious choice of these core values on the life you live such as; achievement, adventure, balance, beauty, common courtesy, challenge, determination, fairness, knowledge, love, loyalty, responsibility, self-respect, service to others, time for family, wisdom, wealth.
   ii. **Personal Goals and Objectives in the Workplace.** Some positivity, personal goals aligned with the company's vision are important for performance improvement and sustenance of job morale examples: greater communication, personal growth, interpersonal skills etc.

   "We're all human, aren't we? Every human life is worth the same, and worth saving."
   - J.K. Rowling

You Give Back to Society and Engage in Community Activity.

We all grew up in the community and benefited from the valuable services done by others ranging from the community market, communal water development project, health clinic among others. It's therefore fair that we become responsible members of the society and give back more than we received from these communities. The purposes and intents shouldn't be a go-getter, but rather *a go-giver*, focusing more on others than you. It's important to have a burning desire to achieve your goals and ambitions, but finding a way to add value to the lives of other people is ultimately mutually beneficial to you as well.

Community engagement is defined as a combined process of working with community groups with an aim of addressing issues that influence the welfare and prosperity of the same group. It may appear contrary to common sense to generously offer your time and money, but this is a worthy investment. Providing for others and becoming of service to the less fortunate helps in bonding with the local community and becoming a part of something larger than yourself. The focus shifts from individuals to communal for inclusivity.

It feels good to participate in the community activities more than just donating money to charitable organizations. You will always receive more than you give to society and that's part of the joy that emanates from engaging in community activity and the reason we should be giving even more to society.

Truly affluent people can attest to this certitude. We are the people who influence the society and change the perspectives of the world and leave it a better place than we found it. The well-off understand the fact that the more you give, the more those good feelings and positive vibes return back to live with you.

> *"The freedom of affluence opposes and contradicts the freedom of community life."*
> *- Wendell Berry*

You Invest in Yourself: The Future Depends on It

Your learning agility becomes your most valued asset and therefore every reason to make a dedication to keep learning on a long-term basis. Take part in sales conference-meetings, road-shows, purchase books, view audio-visual content, podcasts etc. A lot of times we fail to invest in ourselves and it turns to be the case of, *"killing the goose that lay the golden egg"*

Pepe Minambo in his book, *The Game Changer*, fully describes the worth of investing in knowledge as outlined in the following extract,

"Nothing has provoked the human mind over centuries like good books, if you had the chance to sit down with any great genius or world changer, you will definitely realize that the bedrock of their success was curved out of an experience with a great book."

Jean-Pierre De Villiers a professional speaker who inspires companies and individuals and has captivated audiences across the UK and abroad to live a healthy and productive life, once said your rituals define the quality of your life in one of his seminars that I attended in Teecom, Media City, Dubai, UAE in 2016. "Early in the morning, it's a good idea to start by giving gratitude to our Heavenly Father. Downing a cup of water lemon afterwards has the effect of alkalizing your body which is a good way to start your day; it helps in combating formation of free radicals known to cause cancer."

How do you invest in yourself and career?

LiveCareer has highlighted the following ways to invest in self that will go a long way in improving the quality of your life.

1. **Enhance Knowledge and Gain New Experience.** Employers offer additional in house-training, you can also supplement it with expert training courses from government bodies, non-governmental and professional organizations, local county colleges, workshops, seminars and through tutors.

2. **Degree and Certifications: To Increase Your Pay and Advance Your Career.** Certifications in your field of endeavor can bolster your undergraduate and post-graduate degrees and increase the chances of a promotion and a possible pay rise. Find the program you seek and enroll today for certifications and academic degrees from accredited online programs, universities, and technical as well as county colleges. Certifications are more valuable when it comes to highly technical careers, whereas for management or business related roles a degree is necessary and becomes a prerequisite to step in the hallway. The relevance of the courses varies in different parts of the world, so it's always good to do your home-work well before embarking on a course.

3. **Career Planning and Preparation.** Simply conduct a career research by accumulating information from libraries, consult a career planner or go on a weekend retreat and brainstorm and optimally tweak an already existing career plan.
4. **Find a Career Coach or Mentor.** Sometimes you need expert guidance up and out on issues pertaining to career, relationship, nutrition and finances.
5. **Create and Grow Your Personal Brand.** Distinguishing yourself from the competition will influence how your customers will perceive you in a crowded market place. It's therefore vital to get a well-done webpage, LinkedIn outline or blog, exhibiting your achievements, expertise, prowess, and capabilities. You never know who will contact you next for big business or provide you with a step up on your career ladder.
6. **Find a Career Mentor: Don't Ask a Stranger.** Making mistakes can be very costly, involve a mentor with the requisite knowledge and expertise to help you set goals, and navigate the all crucial path to success.
7. **What to Expect From Creating Extra-Ordinary Relationships.** Your personal relationships outweighs your circumstances and the unique fact still remains that real success hinges on establishing and maintaining great relationships. Every reason we should not assume our professional contacts. We should leverage on networking events, seminars and workshops, trade fairs and exhibitions, participation in walks, charitable and community events to regularly oil our networks. Let's not leave it to chance, it's harder to resuscitate a relationship when you have lost your job or fallen out of business as people can read through you when your intents and purposes are not so very genuine.

Ultimate Thoughts: Investing in Yourself is Investing in Your Career

I want to wrap it up here with *three investments* which reach the threshold of not just being sufficient but also necessary to reach your pinnacle of success. They have the effect of raising your levels of confidence, precision, focal-point, power and authority.

a) **Take time to Invest in Your Self-discovery.** The well-to-do persons can attest to this simple fact. This is the long and circuitous journey of comprehending yourself, your ambitions, fortifying your strengths and working-on and fine-tuning blind spots (trouble areas) invigorated through positive feedback. The Harvard Business Review depicts that real leader's work very hard to grow self-awareness through a series of unrelenting and spirited self-exploration.

b) **Successful Habits: Acquire One Each Day** After self-discovery this exercise catapults your expertise from conceptual to a habit that sways things in your favor. You can begin with a morning routine that will motivate you for the rest of the day e.g. listening to a podcast on personal growth on your way to work.

c) **It's All About Communication Skills.**

"Success is 15% due to professional knowledge and 85% due to the ability to express ideas, to assume leadership, and to arouse enthusiasm among people."
- Dale Carnegie

Poor communication has been sighted as the greatest drawback and what most CEO's complain about, that their professionals lack to initiate prosperity, influence and steer their teams forward in the right direction.

It's better late than never, begin your Investment TODAY and reap the consequent benefits in due course.

"Education is the most powerful weapon which you can use to change the world."
- Nelson Mandela

Laban T. M'mbololo, Esq.

Amplify Your Business

23 days of prospecting

In order to drum for more business it is important that salespeople spend a lot of time prospecting. Like a successful golfer devotes time selflessly to practice in order to perform well in a golf tournament, it follows that a successful salesperson needs to invest quality time in prospecting for potential customers in order to have a great sales career and never hit a dry-spell of sales leads.

Below herein I have outlined the "Bible" of Prospecting;

Day 1 – Turn Your Smartphone and Phone Book into a Sales Tool
Turn to your smartphone and pull out contacts of possible prospects. You will be amazed at how many known-contacts you had overlooked and could easily approach, schedule appointments and book business straight away. Here's another secret: phone prospecting is more prone to success since many of your competitors are leveraging more on mails. The backdrop of emails is that if the addresses are not current they will bounce back, while many more get unanswered or the recipients just don't bother to respond.

Day 2 – Routine Payment Recipients

Be sure to compile and take inventory of persons to whom you pay on a weekly or monthly basis. For starters, list your grocer, service station operator, the cashiers at the electric, gas, or Telephone Company, your hairstylist etc.

Day 3 – Infrequent Payment Recipients

Create a register of the people you make payments to intermittently. These will include your jeweler, painter, carpet cleaner, pharmacist, lawn-care contractor, clothing store owner, furniture dealer, car dealer, mechanic etc.

Day 4 – Professional Services Payments Beneficiaries

More often than not you seek professional services. You deal with professional people quite frequently such as doctors, dentists, psychologists, specialists and if you have school going children you have had to deal with lecturers, teachers, bursars and tutors. Other professionals include attorneys (lawyers and advocates), accountants, architects, consultants, bankers, and the clergy, imam and realtor or property agent.

Day 5 – Organizations You Belong To

What about the church, temple or mosque where you worship? The clubs, hotels, societies, religious organizations, professional organizations, governmental and non-governmental organizations, and associations you deal with regularly. Create tabulation and populate a list of all the people you know, deal with or are members of these organizations. Include their names, location and if necessary e-mail addresses and phone numbers.

Day 6 – References and Social Associates

These are people you have socially interacted with presently or in the past. Make a list of their names – present and past employers, employees, co-workers, teachers, physicians, they are a prime source for prospecting. Also, don't forget as many of your neighbors as possible from all the neighborhoods' since childhood.

Day 7 – Old School Friends in Academy, College, University and Classmates

Find your school mates, friends and colleagues who you attended classes and probably graduated together. Take inventory of other professional classes, debating clubs, toastmasters club, baking class, dressmaking class who live in your surroundings.

Day 8 – Family and Relatives

How about your family and relatives and those of your spouse? You already have a great deal of information about them, and they can be approached under favorable circumstances.

Day 9 – Organizations Your Spouse Belongs To

Take inventory and enlist all possible members that belong to your significant other's organizations. These can include members of her health club, sports team, business association, organized groups etc. Target her circle of influence of social associates which you could approach as possible business prospects. NB: don't prejudge their needs or values. Call each one of them and see what happens.

Day 10 – Recreation, Leisure and Sports Contacts

Refer to friends, acquaintances and colleagues you mingle with in biking, bowling, golf, football, basketball, netball, tennis, badminton or cricket clubs whom you could contact and consider doing business with. Consider also members of other passive leisure, hobbies and sports you engage with e.g. playing chase, scrabble, ludo, puzzles.

Day 11 – Military Friends, Troops, Service Men, Armed Forces

Whether you were once a retired soldier or not you had met and come across and known about the names of the men and women you have come to know through military service such as military spouses and kids and through events such as coalitions, support groups, military friends associations, military foundations or memorials for fallen heroes. It could also be through visiting friends and relatives at the military canteen and supermarket store at the military barracks for purchase of discounted food items, fuel, drinks and beverages.

Day 12 – Present Clients

Inform all your clients on the recent products, modifications, latest editions and reviews, product attributes as well as new services that could generate interest and make them offers so as to generate more repeat business.

Day 13 – Newlyweds or Newly Married Couples

Make a point of populating a list of weddings that took place in the previous month by paying a visit to your local library or newspaper office, or by going through the local newspapers and magazines, local church records. Most church weddings, newspaper or online announcements will give the couples address or even possibly their places of work.

Day 14 – Sales Canvassing and Cold Calls

This forms an integral part of any organization's sales strategy. This method is outdated because more often than not it targets the people who are unlikely to make a purchase from you. Nevertheless, it doesn't hurt once in a month to cold canvass by making first-time-telephone calls to prospects or consumer door-to-door marketing by knocking all doors in offices and residential apartments. This could probably trigger some interest and find you some new clients. In a stormy or very hot weather, cold canvassing in large apartment complexes will suffice.

Day 15 – Referrals

Make a list of 100 friends, existing customers, colleagues and associates and you could also extend it to your new and old LinkedIn contacts. Phone each one of them and request at least five references that you could possibly engage in phone calls or by arranging visitations. This method is guaranteed to work well if you use the friend's name at the point of contacting the referees especially if they have an existing close relationship or had a fruitful dealing in the past.

Day 16 – New Business Owners

Search through recent newspapers and magazines in the business section, this time reading the legal notices of people starting new businesses.

Day 17 – Promotions and Transfers

Make another list from the past months newspapers, magazines and periodicals of professionals who have received promotions or who are being transferred to your area.

Day 18 – Business Cards

Rummage and delve into your business card collection or business card holder. Scour for Senior Management, Vice-President and CEO's contacts especially the ones known personally to you or through friends, colleagues and associates who can make an introduction on your behalf. This is because these are decision makers and will make instantaneous decisions or guide you correctly along the corporate corridors where you can get assistance and book business quickly.

Day 19 – New Homeowners

Home purchasers' whether new or existing enter the list of prospects. Contact local estate agents or property managers and check warranty deeds listed in the newspaper.

Day 20 – Prior Cancellations

Filter through your old diaries. Populate a list of all the prospects you either made calls or visited who cancelled and possibly postponed appointments with you, and were never rescheduled and followed through. Give them a call and see whether their situations have since changed or establish if they are still interested in your products and services.

Day 21 – The House or Business Next Door

Contact your client's next door neighbor or business. Introduce yourself and the valuable business that you offer, and ask whether you can be of service. You are already in the neighborhood, so this would be a convenient time to discover and develop new clients.

Day 22 – Build Your Agency

Make a list of the people you contacted this month that you would like to recruit to your agency. Give the names to your general manager or sales manager and perhaps an appointment would result. You have the opportunity not only to recommend your friends as associates, but to watch your business and your agency grow.

Day 23 – Connect With the Greater Community

Utilize contacts from the security meetings with community leaders, community welfare meetings, community development meetings, charitable work, freedom from hunger walk to build your own and start connecting with the wider community and tap into a sea of endless opportunities.

Epilogue

You are Now a Power Seller!

You have learned how to attract customers and keep them coming, how to get value out of your niche clients who bring you 80% of your revenue, how to strategically position yourself in the market place, brand and sell yourself.

This is it, what's left is to put it into gainful practice in the real world. This needs you to believe. An outcome of any incident, state of affairs or circumstances you encounter in your lifetime is determined by whether you believe the thing can visibly take shape or otherwise. This concept is referred to as **The Power of Belief** (or **Non-Belief**). This therefore calls for you to have an inner conviction in the products and/or services you are pushing or offering. Notwithstanding your product knowledge, it's important to believe in the products and services you are selling, your sales techniques, and the company you represent. More importantly believe in yourself by showing confidence in your dealings with your prospects and customers, *the buck stops with you!*

Remember customers buy YOU long before buying your products and services and therefore you will need to demonstrate belief that will make the prospects and customers buy from you and not the competition.

You have the power to achieve what your mind sets out to achieve, you are now a *Power Seller* …get out there and prove your worth.

www.ingramcontent.com/pod-product-compliance
Lightning Source LLC
Chambersburg PA
CBHW020445220526
45464CB00002B/860